By the book «Guide on successful ideas: Information for those who are building a new life: Part I & II» we open a series of works united by the common name "Own Land". It was made by the efforts of a group of authors and translators from different countries and cities connected by common views and interests of the online community OMELA. Due to their work, as well as to the management of the editor-in-chief and author Artur Captan, in 2017 this project was successfully completed and translated from Polish and Russian languages.

We invite everyone to participate in the OMELA community projects. The following books from this series will have the pilot titles "Sad truth about the modern world" and "100 ideas for the enlightened state". All questions on cooperation, information placement, as well as the desire to subscribe to the following books of the series, please send to ruhavik.sakret09@gmail.com with the note "Own Land".

Artist, journalist and traveler Artur Captan was born in the family of creative intellectuals in 1969 in Poznan (Poland). For a long time he lived with his parents who immigrated to Canada, but in 2005 he moved to the land of his ancestors, where he took an active part in the projects of various "green" themes. In his search for interesting material, he visited various countries and wrote hundreds of articles on various and pressing problems, for which he rightly can be called a "citizen of the planet Earth." The ways of the online community of OMELA and journalist Artur Captan crossed in 2016, and the fruit of this event was the book you see before you.

This book from the series "Own Land" was prepared and edited with the assistance and support of the private printing initiative Sekret Polishinel Ltd. Under the general guidance of Artur Captan, for which we express our special gratitude.

GUIDE ON SUCCESSFUL IDEAS: INFORMATION FOR THOSE WHO ARE BUILDING A NEW LIFE

+ BONUS !

Table of contents:

PART I: "IMMERSION"

Have you already swallowed the pill of master Neo? You want to find out how deep the rabbit whole is. The imposed world of ready-made solutions, stores, ready-made recipes from banks and offices, greedy for our money, "smart" officials and other sharks of business and politics, who are so fond of their problems' transferring onto our shoulders?

No, the rabbit-hole is not deep at all. Perhaps, the answer is on the surface. Now you will think about this any time your hand trying to reach your wallet. You will be very surprised, as I was, when coming to the simple finding that all you need for happiness is right under our feet! In addition, it is cheap!

You know, each of us belongs to the human community. Yes, you belong to the Homo sapiens species - "a rational man". In turn, the society of the similar biped one are treat us loyal less, and are indifferent to us in most cases, and if they provide us with ready-made solutions for life, it's not for nothing. It takes away our time and efforts exhausting our resources. Let us be honest, the society does not give a damp about us and about our condition, about either we are happy or not, either we are smart or stupid. They have already left us to get out safely of this toilet hole called the life. Because the benefit may be derived from any our interest or needs, and we, after all, do the same. Because, damn it, each of us want to get out of the rat race! However, there was the Tree of Life in the midst of the Paradise, not only Tree of Knowledge of Good and Evil. (Genesis 2-9). We remember the taste of its fruit, or was it just a dream?

So, to pay or not to pay – is that Shakespeare's question? This question is similar to the point of honour - a man's question, which is called "are you able to stick up for yourself?" "If I don't stand my ground, how will I find a way out of this maze?" (the song "Dogs" by Pink Floyd) Because we are not the gears in Moloch's wheel "debt - money - debt - time ..." We will work together to find a way out of this tunnel! And God help us.

"And the rest - keep out of trouble, and they will not reach you" - as one wise Hobbit said.

So, welcome to the wonderful world of the OMELA community! Here you will find some fascinating discoveries and also some little lifehacks, and you will hardly pass them by. They will help you to see new horizons and will assist the person that has skilful hands and a smart head!

***Chapter 1.** We build easy - from clay, lime and sand, from bales of straw according to the StrawBale technology, from wood and logs' scraps, from hemp waste. The real houses for little money – isn't it what you dreamed about?*

Nowadays construction of houses from bales of straw, clay and sand, scraps of wood and also sacks with soil seems something frivolous, superficial and even fantastic as if the dwelling of some "hobbits". "Do we know your straw!" – the inhabitant will tell with a smile and he will be wrong – in all these materials huge potential is hidden.

Ease, simplicity and availability (cost) of the materials – these are the indisputable benefits of similar designs. Plus resistance to adverse conditions of the external environment – it is known, for example, that the oldest house built according to the StrawBale technology in France exists within about 300 years without any visible destructions. The material for construction grows just on the fields. To get a straw in bales rather ordinary sheave binding machine from the former GDR is necessary – one day, and "bricks" for the whole house are ready!

"All new is well forgotten old" - one proverb says. And this is true. And what kind of experience we got from our "great-grandfathers"? For more than one thousand years in Ukraine clay houses are known under the name "mazanka", which walls consist of a mixture of clay, sand

and straw, and the foundations raised only 30-40 cm over the earth level. Walls were covered with a thick layer of the mixture containing lime, clay and a cow dung and then those layers were carefully bleached. Those were small, cozy and fireproof houses without any unpleasant smells but with fine heat-insulating characteristics. Walls in such constructions "breathes" – the usage of only natural materials didn't create any obstacles for air exchange between the external environment and internal space of the house.

Due to the course of physics, we know that the best isolation from cold penetration is the air layer, so-called "porosity" of material. Under a microscope, it is possible to differentiate that clay consists of tiny plates which are placed like "piles" as if sheets of paper in the book, between which straw "pipes", also containing a lot of air, are placed. Whatever was applied to fill an internal cavity of walls – clay with sand, straw, waste after hemp production (the reference on Cohabitat: https://www.cohabitat.net) – what riches one has – all this was preserved between two thick plaster coats from all directions that absolutely excluded a possibility of mold and fungi appearance caused by the moisture penetration, either as appearance of insects and rodents, and also fire. On one video the worker takes the heated gas torch behind such a wall within five minutes – and there is no ignition! With the advent of various construction materials such technology "faded into the background", mainly because it is simpler to build from ready blocks (bricks, slag stones, gas-silicates), probably, than to prepare building mixture from clay and straw. Better to say, the industry of ready construction materials won. And this is good! Because the combination of the advanced building technologies with the experience of our ancestors will provide us truly amazing results! If, of course, you don't live in conditions, so adverse that the massive house totally from steel concrete building is the only correct exit from the current situation. So, we will try to approach this question with the maximum objectivity and we will consider all pluses and minuses of such a project:

- The cost and availability of a building material – got grade "Excellent". All necessary for a building is often placed under one's legs. It isn't necessary to go to the shop.

- In such houses it is cool in summer heat and heat in severe frosts thanks to heat-insulating properties of materials the house is made of. Besides, straw bales are an excellent barrier for sounds. In such houses it is silent, even near the brisk street.

Now we will consider the expenses of efforts, time and our precious health.

Surely the question is rather disputable. Not all build as Chinese does – a multi-storey skyscraper within few months. But the crew of skilled workers with huge experience in StrawBale technology (for example, Cohabitat) copes with an individual residential cottage of 100 sq.m. approximately within three weeks. With songs and jokes in three days a working basis with a framework (a facade under a roof) is ready as a rule. At the end of the building there are two buckets of rubbish in the form of ashes – a dream of the most advanced ecologist!

Such houses successfully stand all possible stability tests – up to a tornado and floods. The straw bale covered with a thick plaster coat is similar in weight with the standard block made of silicate with gas forming additives. One Belarus civil engineering firm ("EKOCYB" Vladimir Krupski: http://ecocube.by) directed further away – it makes standard straw blocks with a special covering – houses from such "eco-cubes" are being gathered like LEGO details. For standard straw blocks on all length of walls special metal probes are exhausted to maintain the high-level rigidity. So, the presence of bearded men with huge wooden beaters on the StrawBale construction is not an exotic at all but the necessity. All heavy and hinged details of a building structure are fastened on a tough wooden framework.

In areas where the possibility of spontaneous disasters is high, surely, the security measures have to be taken. In the case of floods, it is necessary to consider methods of excess water removal from the basis of walls using pile and other supporting frameworks. When the house is placed behind a wood nevertheless the probability of the fire is minimal – clay doesn't flare up.

The durability of buildings is caused also by rather high seismostability of the construction and also by the fact that moisture content up to 20% doesn't cause straw rotting processes.

Now the candy for sceptics. Most people will tell you that such a building technology isn't supported by modern practice at all, it has no the approved regulations and no rules, therefore, it is doomed to failure. This is only partially truth, and the true part is very small. In Poland, for example, to the 50th years of last century, quite legally there were state standards and regulations on similar technologies. Rummaging the building history manuals you will find this information.

If we have convinced you of something …

The first rule of the movement's participant says – "never get despaired because despondency is the most terrible sin". Of course, we aren't idealists, and we perfectly understand that without expanses even dog box can't be built. Then let's take the calculator in our hand and begin to calculate:

- expanses for a box construction, as a rule, consume about 30 - 40% of a total cost of building construction. Another part of expenses is an internal finishing, communications, the equipment, an interior and the landscape beautification – the things that make our life more comfortable. It should be considered when forming the budget of a building. The construction of the house from natural materials (clay, sand, straw), as a rule, costs 3.5-5 times cheaper, than in the case of a construction from "classical" materials.

- The weakest spot in the building according to the StrawBale technology is weather, to be exact - an atmospheric precipitation in the form of a rain or snow. In blocks that were not enough dried rotting, a mold and other undesirable phenomena can appear. It is even possible that such blocks won't live up to the process of building and the quicker we will hide them under a canopy or the shelter, it is better. Therefore, after the construction of the foundation and a wooden framework it is necessary to think at once of the roof arrangement – perhaps, the most difficult, expensive and labor-consuming part of the project.

- For the rest the approximate algorithm of actions for the construction of inexpensive environmentally friendly and reliable own house as "mazanka" looks as follows:

- First of all, outline the project of what you want to receive as a result. You can bravely draw the rounded corners and oval rooms, creating a curvilinear facade. Ready construction projects can be found on the Internet on OpenResourse pages. Of course, the help of the skilled design engineer and masters is required.

- o Define the site where construction is planned to be build. The soil where ground waters lie deeply from a surface is more preferable. Anyway, take care of cutting moisture from the future foundation, for example, by means of a drainage pillow from gravel.

- o Plane the site under the future construction.

- o Dig a trench along the perimeter of the planned building on the depth of 0.75 m for zones of a temperate climate. If you live in cold regions, then the depth of frost penetration in the soil will be more, so and the trench should be dug more deeply.

- o If you are going to do the tape type foundation of concrete, then establish a timbering from boards on the trench width (about 50 cm) and height from earth level – about 40 cm. If on your site the soil is rather dense, it is possible to make the foundation of a natural stone and cement mortar.

- o After the foundation is ready, you move to the creation of a wooden framework for all future house construction. The optimal thickness of walls is 30 cm.

- o Define where the main construction materials will be obtained. Clay can be bought, or it is possible to get it on your own. Good clay is defined simply – wet a clay lump, roll from it a sausage and curtail it a ring. The most viscous clay won't leave big cracks in such a ring – and consequently, is the most suitable for construction. Otherwise, it is necessary to add cement or quicklime to the sand. As a filler it is possible to use straw, flax, hemp waste, buckwheat pod and also large wood sawdust.

For the preparation of working mix it will be approximately required: 2 parts of sand, 1 part of clay, 0.6 parts of straw. Add a little water that it was possible to stick together from them several balls with a diameter of 2 cm. Then throw them from height of at least a meter: if the lump was scattered it is necessary to add water and/or clay; if it was flattened out – add sand and/or straw. Your task is to pick up such proportions that the lump kept the form having fallen from the height.

- o To prepare the building mixture, it is convenient to use the hole laid by a tarpaulin. Put components in a hole and trample down by means of your legs until the mixture becomes uniform.

- o Stamp clay and straw mixture in the framework created from firrings.

- o For the purpose of additional winterization, it is possible to make a reed firrings all perimeter's long.

- o Plaster the house outside with a mixture of lime and sand (1:1 or 1:2). A plaster coat – 2.5 – 3 cm.

- o Plaster walls inside with the mixture of clay and sand (1:3 or 1:4).

- o Don't forget about the construction of a roof! Any option will be suitable for this purpose. The main rule is to avoid heavy designs.

A small turn of a plot or:

"How to build the house of bags filled with soil: the brief guide on Earthbag technology"

Houses from bags filled with soil are rather "fresh" idea. The house, built according to such a technology, is really similar to the dwelling of gnomes or hobbits. A basis of a construction material – soil, clay and bags. Such bags in case of desire can be found on dumps, it is possible to purchase in building stores or enterprises. It will be very good if you manage to find long "pipes" from polypropylene fabric – such "sausages" will allow to create rounded-off construction easily and quickly.

So, what is required in case of a construction on Earthbag technology:

1. polypropylene bags;

2. soil for filling the bags;

3. clay for an external and inside layer of plaster;

4. the metal gauze for an armor of walls and the foundation;

5. boards for a roof design, and also for doorway and window opening;

6. a film for a roof;

7. a cardboard for a roof;

8. ropes for the fixture of roof beams;

9. a pipe for water drainage;

10. stones, small crushed stone, gravel for filling of the foundation;

11. bags filled with cement for the foundation (the first two rows).

When above-mentioned building materials are prepared, it is possible to start the building process.

First of all, the superficial trench under the foundation where the pipe for water drainage is put has to be dug out. Then the trench is filled up with stones and filling brick. After that on a plain surface begins the setting of walls made of bags. The first two rows are bags with cement. Further – the metal gauze. Then – bags with the soil that are shifted by the metal gauze or logs, boards, etc each two rows. to achieve reliable fixing of bags. After three rows of bags (2 rows of cement and 1 row of the soil) are laid, the doorway is arranged then setting the bags with the soil continues. In the same way it will be necessary to arrange the window openings made of tree. Approximately for 5 levels, without reaching a roof, it will be necessary to lay ropes which then will be tied to roof beams, creating thus a roofing construction fixing.

The construction of a roof consists of wooden rafters which are covered with a cardboard layer, and from above a dense film is placed which will protect from a rain well. In such houses the good decision will be the form of a housing structure which is narrowed to top similar to the principle of a cone. The house is plastered by clay mixture within and outside, and then painted, or a layer of the lime diluted in water with the addition of the painting pigment is being put. For the creation of an original design, it is possible to use ordinary glass bottles. The entrance arch made of adobe and glass color bottles looks wonderful! And besides, it reminds about pleasantly spent days…☺

Of course, the house built of bags with soil has no ideally straight lines. It differs rather with uniqueness and ascertaining of the fact of a huge break in the direction to freedom. And the softness of smooth lines is exactly that is necessary for the circulation of Universe energy in your house – Tzi (according to the Chinese doctrine Feng-Shui).

One more idea for the most advanced one, or the story about how one Dude rummaged on a trash dump very successfully:

How to build the house of soil and tires: the brief guide on Earthships technology:

Houses made according to this technology are constructed similarly to houses of bags with the soil. However, instead of bags, old tires and also cans or glass bottles are used here. All this material can be found on dumps! Besides that you build the house without any expanses, you also do the environment a little more pure. The first house according to this technology was built by Mike Reynalds in 1970. Nowadays this technology is successfully used in England, Spain, Portugal, Belgium. Such houses are characterized by durability, aseismic stability and heat saving properties.

For the foundation constructing it is necessary to do deepening in the ground which depth corresponds to a width of a tire and settle a layer of tires which then is carefully filled up with soil, but it is better - with crushed stone (gravel) mixed up with sand, carefully rammed. Then a film is settled for providing of a waterproofing. If construction has several floors, the armor is necessary. From above the wooden beams are established that is necessary for a floor creation.

The house facade made according to the Earthships technology is done of tires which cavity is filled with soil, and space between tires is filled with the mixture of clay. Tires are settled in chessboard manner. For the creation of inner room partitions cans or glass bottles, clay and sand mixture are used.

The main concept of such building says: the less energy is required to turn the found object into a useful construction material, the better. Such an idea got the name "embodied-energy" or "smart idler".

 The similar principles are suitable also for construction of the house from straw bales. In this case a plant remains acts as the main building material: flax, hemp, wheat, and also the pressed dry hay. The ideal option is the eddish (dry stalks) from rye conversion. Rye straw isn't in favor of mice – therefore it will be what is necessary for us. It is better to take the waste created by a sheaf binder (which is tied up with a twine) – they have a convenient rectangular shape.

The sequence of actions in case of a building process will be a bit different:

The foundation construction:

- o Creation of a framework.

- o Roof construction to avoid ingress of rain water into the middle of the arranged walls.

- o Filling the framework intervals with straw bales, which are imposed with "bandaging" as bricks in brickwork. Ranks of bales are fixed together by metal probes.

- o Straw "shaving", for example, by means of the chainsaw. Walls become smoother.

- o Putting a plaster coat on a basic grid (thickness – up to 7, 5 cm). Plaster mix consists of sand, clay and water. The addition of lime or cement will be useful (1-2 trowels on a bucket of working mix). To increase moisture protective properties add linseed oil and to avoid the clothes' soiling in the case of contact with a plaster coat it is recommended to add the flour paste to the last plaster coat.

The houses' made of a straw facade are, as a rule, a plaster with the addition of various pigments of different colors. However, painting of facades of straw houses has its specifics: the applied paint shall be vapor-permeable. That is moisture which comes out from within shouldn't get into a "trap" and remain in walls as it can cause straw rotting sooner or later. Therefore it is impossible to apply oil paints to the painting of facades of such houses. It is admissible to use latex paints on a water basis in case that it is a quality product with a high degree of vapor permeability. Allow walls "to breathe" also silicone paints, however, the price of them is rather high.

To create an attractive facade of the eco-friendly house is rather simple to prepare limy paint on your own. Such a way of finishing was used many years ago. All that is required for such paint creation is lime, water, little salt, drying oils and alkaliproof pigments of any color. Such covering is moisture resistant and frosts and doesn't soil clothes in case of contact.

3 dangers for the straw:

Fire: The reliable method of a construction's fire resistance increase is a treatment of every straw bale with the mixture of clay by a short-term putting the bale into the mixture, a dusting or putting several layers of clay over the straw manually. The general part of clay in such kind of treatment will constitute up to 10%. Such block will be a bit heavier and the process of drying will require some time, but it is very reliable method to protect the dwelling from the fire.

Moisture: Straw is afraid only of the long impact of moisture but short-term is not as it possesses a natural capability to evaporate excessive moisture. And straw "breathes" better, than a tree. However, to minimize a moisture entry on a facade, it is necessary to design the straw house so that eaves supported the level of walls at least than on 60 cm.

Rodents: In order to rodents not become your closest neighbors, it is necessary to pour straw piles with the slaked lime while arranging the walls' construction. Rye straw also won't be tasty to them.

How to make a roof of straw and clay: Such design costs not much, but demands observance of some requirements:

- o a roof bias – not less than 40-50 □;

- o massive rafters from poles 50-70 mm thick;

- o poles have to lean on peg from solid tree breeds which are inserted into the rafters' holes of 60-70 mm depth;

- o the ends of poles are fastened with nails;

- o for poles do not cave in on an attic floor it is necessary to establish props which can be moved after full drying of a roof;

- o it is necessary to cover both slopes simultaneously: 1-2 rows on one side and 1-2 rows on another for not to overload a rafter.

Working with straw:

- o Not too tight bales with a diameter of 10-20 cm are tied up, length – 50-100 cm. Ears at the same time are surely chopped off. Sheaves are placed horizontally from the edge to the skate. Edges of the subsequent bales have to block partially edge of previous, forming a layer of 10-15 cm thickness. Every time when the bale is laid, it is untied and flattered. Through each 3-4 layers the straw is "combed" by means of rake then it is filled in with clay mixture, which is smoothed by means of a shovel to make the roof flat. After the first layer become dry, the second one is filled in and it is also carefully flattered with a shovel. It is necessary for not to give any chance to destructive moisture stay in roughness's of the roof surface.

Working with clay: The clay used for mix has to be rather fat, with the content of sand no more, than 15%. In order to make work with clay simpler, it should be friable. It is possible to prepare clay for the winter period: it will be chilled and will get the necessary properties. The clay volume which will be required for a roof can be calculated: on 30-35 sq.m of walls' surface about 1 m3 of clay is required.

The clay has to be:

- filled up into the hole covered with tarpaulin, approximately 10-15 cm layer;

- filled in with water: 1 parts of clay and 2 parts of water;

- sustained not less than 5 hours;

- mixed, trying to get uniformity of paste.

The straw will help to define suitability of the received mixture. It is put into the mixture: if the straw for some period of time has kept the vertical position, it means that the mixture is suitable for usage, if at once has fallen, it is necessary to add some clay.

Several words about a design of StrawBale:

Internal finishing of houses from natural materials assumes the availability of warm, pastel colors and not striking coloring of furniture which shall emphasize the "natural" style of the device of an interior easily. The rounded corners, niches, twisted ladders and the energy center of all composition – a big fireplace or the furnace. The rest, as people say – a matter of taste. But the small frame with a glass through which one can see that the house is really built of straw bales is already more likely a tradition of StrawBale. Such "Windows of the truth" are very popular in the USA. In the conclusion there is a small Bonus Trek for those who have read this chapter up to the end.

How to build the house of firewood and clay: the brief guide on Cordwood technology

The economic method of own housing building is offered also by Cordwood technology which provides a building of the house from clay and scraps of wood (firewood). Such technology was approved also recently. Perhaps, preparation of components for creation of such construction will be the most labor-consuming part of this building, as they shall be approximately of equal length and thickness. However, if the device like a woodchopper is at your disposal, then the task considerably becomes simpler.

Benefits of houses from logs and clay:

> o an opportunity to build the construction quickly;
>
> o good thermal insulation;
>
> o aseismic stability and durability of a construction;
>
> o the simplicity of a construction

That is, in fact, this technology has the same advantages, as StrawBale one, however, the basic difference consists in the next moments:

> o if you live near the wood or the carving wood is available for you, then such a construction

will be rather cheap for you. If the main component of such a construction is unavailable for you, then the house from other natural materials will be a preferable option;

- o houses from scraps obligatory have to be either treated by a fire-retarding agent, or some protective coatings or plasters are to laid on all the walls' surface. Otherwise, the risk of the fire considerably increases;

- o houses from firewood and clay weigh more than straw one, so the foundation will be required more massive;

- o before the building is started, a log (firewood) is very desirable to be impregnated with insecticides as wreckers can do considerable harm to the construction. Then material needs to be checked and dried carefully. Otherwise from such a house not only your cat will run away.

Some nuances of a Cordwood building: In order that construction turned out an esthetic one, reliable and durable, adhere the following recommendations:

- o the wood used for the construction has to be dry, otherwise wood may crack;

- o it is obligatory to delete all bark from a tree because wreckers settle exactly there, and rotting process can begin;

- o packs have to be at least about 35 cm long;

- o walls need to be arranged as a woodpile, that is on corners each row of adjacent walls goes with an overlap with each other;

- o every 50-70 cm of a laying need to be done a binding of inch boards;

- o it is possible to settle 3 rows at once, then it is necessary to take a pause(about a day) for the wall to become dried;

- o to make the house warmer, leave an emptiness in the internal space of walls – subsequently, they can be filled with a heater or sawdust;

- o try to create the facade as flat as possible. For this purpose use a board, for example, from plywood or boards. When you do a laying of walls, use a board, moving it in the process of levels stacking up;

- o the waterproofing of the foundation have to be of very high quality;

- o if you plan several floors, then beams of overlapping have to rest one party on an external wall, and the second – on a framework of an internal partition.

At the end there are some figures:

- o a ratio of clay mixture and logs – 1:4;

o a ratio of straw which is recommended to be added to clay mixture - about 1:9;

o optimal depth of the foundation – 50 cm.

We listed the main technologies of a nonconventional building in this chapter that are known to us for today. If you know some other, or you have invented your own one, please, write us: ruhavik.sakret09@gmail.com «OMELA–Belarus».

Chapter 2: The most necessary gadget for today. We print our future on the printer.

Sometimes in the evening, when the sky overhead clears up, and the silence around becomes almost crystal, I wonder - what is a person compared to this entire world order? We face such a scale that hardly fit in our heads - what the eye contemplates is a tiny flower in a huge bouquet, and then begins a whole, vast meadow... And if you represent the constellations as a complex mechanism of denticles and gears, then what greatness should the Great Watchmaker possess arranging this all?

By virtue of his natural vanity, a person places himself in the second place after the Creator, but whether he possesses similar talents is another question. Observing all this magnificence, I involuntarily caught myself thinking that for a long time we and the Creator will be on different edges of the intellectual abyss.

A man believed in his greatness, probably, since he has begun to surround himself with the world of things invented for his well-being and comfort. We redesigned nature to suit our needs and grew into the world of our artifacts. Our women have arranged our aspirations, like an old coat to their figure - in the guise of a good goal to simplify everything and make everyone happy. But, I believe, we give more time desired for the reality - a sweet deception and threshold, beyond which there is only the unknown. And yet, looking at all this beautifully arranged world, this luxury of life forms, I want to believe that our Creator does not look like a miserable miser who has withheld from an unfortunate humanity a pair of shekels of immortality. Indeed he does not have any money at all!

"Evil is the ignorance of good," the ancient Greek philosopher Socrates exclaimed, studying the world of people. What a blessing that he did not live up to our days. Any other sane would simply be amazed by watching this orgy of squandering. These insane conflicts that erase cities that have stood for centuries, like a dirty rag takes crumbs from a table. International corporations and governments of countries seem to compete among themselves in an absurd game called "who will more quickly spend and mislead our natural resources." Oh, be damned, this age-old speculation on human weaknesses!

But it's enough of these lyrical digressions because the revolution in the world of things has long been ripe. It, like the first sprout, just broke through the soil, caught by her first antenna and straightened the first stalk. So the giant sequoia is born from a tiny seed - eclipsing in a thousand years half of the forest.

The history of this invention began almost as fun or someone's whim. The fact is that since the mid-1990s, billions of consumers around the world are no longer satisfied with serial stamps produced in huge factories in many millions of copies. The people demanded an exclusive product - and the competitors bent out to satisfy all the wishes of customers, taking into account the unique design and keeping an acceptable price. Marketers of batch production were the first to ring bells as they have noticed a decrease in the volume of sales. But modern concerns are not flexible enough to rebuild the entire technological chain of production in a short time. Ultimately, the companies found that the development of forms, patterns and prototypes for newer and newer models is very expensive.

This was the birth of the small-scale production era - the FabLab program started in the Media Lab at the Massachusetts Institute of Technology, as well as numerous cooperatives in China or India. These small compact workshops, equipped with the most necessary for work, were integrated into whole networks (via the Internet) - the so-called FabFi project, successfully implemented in Afghanistan, Kenya, US and several other countries. They exist on the principles of self-sufficiency and even are able to beat serial production due to the so-called *negative scale effect* and energy reduction.

The FabLab manufacturing has the flexibility, mobility and upgradeability - in short, everything necessary to create single high-tech devices and other products. Ways to organize such production is taught on a popular course in MIT (MAS.863) which is called "How to do (almost) everything."

Standard fab lab is equipped with various types of cutters and plotters (laser, plasma, water jet, knife for cutting sheet materials), three-axis milling and turning machines with computer numerical control, equipment for creating printed circuit boards and prototypes, workstations for testing digital electronics etc., devices controlled via computer in the single technological process.

The most useful in this "gentleman's kit" are, perhaps, universal CNC machines and their subsequent evolution or transformation into a device, which I wanted to tell more in detail.

This design resembles a trick with a hat and a rabbit that you just cannot undo. Watching for it's work is an exciting activity, which, it seems, will never get bored. Initially, the parameters of a certain model are loaded from the software, and soon the print head on a special substrate begins to gravel after a grain of caked plastic to build a figure of the famous Jedi - Master Iodo in natural, three-dimensional form. On the side or front of the device, there is a reel of material resembling a fishing line. It serves as a "fuel" for the printer, like ink in an oldie antediluvian 2-D inkjet printer.

This machine does not have a long story and it has very promising opportunities. I'll venture to notice that the fairy tale about the "magic wand" that can turn a pumpkin into a carriage has never been so close. But it all begins back in 1948 when the American Charles Hull developed a technology for layer-by-layer growth of physical three-dimensional objects from photopolymers. However, the patent for his invention - a device working on new technology - Hull received only in 1986. Then he founded the company 3D System and produced a 3D printing device called Stereolithography Apparatus. The first modification of this machine, widely used then, was the SLA-250 model developed in 1988. The device grew a computer-modeled three-dimensional object from liquid polymers, depositing them layer by layer on a moving platform. Of course, it was not yet the first 3D printer in the modern sense, but it was the model that determined its basic working principle: namely, that objects are being built up gradually, layer by layer.

Since the middle of the 90s of the last century, this technology has begun to develop both in depth and in breadth. For its implementation, virtually all branches of modern science are connected, carrying out 3-D print in various ways and materials. Currently, there are already about 8 types and 12 different technologies used in the device - from stationary desktop devices that can be used in everyday life - from a couple of thousand dollars to huge building and mobile installations worth several million.

Devices for 3D print are distinguished by the following types of workflows:

o Extrusion method: Fused deposition modeling, FDM and Robocasting or Direct Ink Writing (DIW). In the first case, solidification of the material occurs during cooling - the print head extrudes drops of heated thermoplastic onto the cooled base. Drops quickly solidify and adhere to each other, forming layers of the future object. In the second, "ink" (usually a special ceramic compound) comes out of the nozzle in a liquid state, but immediately take the desired form due to its properties.

- o Exposure of photopolymers: laser stereolithography (SLA) and SLA-DLP. In the first version, the ultraviolet laser illuminates the liquid photopolymer (through a photographic pattern, or gradually, a pixel by pixel). In the case of SLA-DLP, the photopolymer is exposed by a special DLP projector.

- o Formation of the object on the prepared powder layer. There are 4 varieties:

- o 3D Printing (3DP) - gluing the powder by applying liquid glue with inkjet printing;

- o Electron-beam melting (EBM) - melting of metal powder by electron beam in vacuum;

- o Selective laser sintering (SLS) and Direct metal laser sintering (DMLS) - melting powder (plastic, metal) under the laser radiation;

- o Selective heat sintering (SHS) - melting powder with a heating head;

- o Electron beam freeform fabrication (EBF) - melting of the feed material in the form of a wire under the electron radiation;

- o Laminated object manufacturing (LOM) - the part is created from a large number of layers of working material, which are gradually superimposed and glued together. Then the laser (or cutting tool) cuts out the contour of the future part;

- o Directed Energy Deposition (DED) - the working material melts under the laser or electron beam;

- o Multi Jet modeling (MJM) - the material is applied by inkjet printing.

Recently, the devices for three-dimensional printing are increasingly used for medical and general building purposes. Therefore, in addition, we can distinguish:

Biological printers are experimental plants in which the 3D structure of the future organ for transplant printing is produced by drops containing living cells. We watched something similar in the French film "The Fifth Element", so now you can see the next phenomenon that came to us from the fantasy world. The application of droplets creates a certain matrix; Further division, growth and modification of cells begins and the final formation of the object takes place. Researchers at Hangzhou Dianzi University have developed a 3D bioprinter called "Regenovo". Already in 2013, Chinese scientists working with a living tissue printed ears, liver and kidneys! True, these organs did not last long - not more than 4 months, because they were deprived of blood vessels. Xu Mingen, the developer of Regenovo, told the world then that "... fully viable printed organs are likely to be created within the next ten to twenty years." In the same year, researchers from the University of Hasselt in Belgium successfully printed a new jaw for an 83 years old Belgian. In early 2016, Kirill Kayem, vice-president of the Skolkovo Science Center (Russia), reported that the native bio-3D printer had printed the thyroid gland for a laboratory mouse, which was then successfully implanted into it. The plans of Russian scientists create a mouse kidney and liver, which will also be implanted in mice.

But this is only the first step towards what the world expects. "Your will lose your head if you find out what results we have achieved so far," said John Craig Venter, one of the foremost specialists in the field of modern bio-technologies, in 2009. In 2010, they were told about the first successful experiments on the creation of artificial living organisms. Venter's group built a living creature literally from information, having studied the DNA of the phi-X174 virus and creating a computer model on the basis of studying the chain of genomes. Further on, there's time for 3D printing installations, that are familiar to us, which some call the "next generation" or 4D. The final material obtained at the output is capable of self-assembly, copying its structure and transformation. "It is very convenient to build living objects of such substances that layer DNA like bricks" - note scientists from the Venter group. According to this technologies, they created an artificial bacterial cage by inserting artificial DNA into it, then they began to observe how the organic form of life synthesized by them moves, feeds, breathes and reproduces itself.

When something like this happens, one cannot help wondering: what did the scientists open this time? A treasure box or a Pandora's Box? It is clear only that a new page has been opened in the knowledge of Life and life forms, and what consequences this knowledge will bring depends on the purity of the hands and the thoughts of their owners. Venter himself reports about his new technology, that "it will first appear in the digital computer world on the basis of digital biology, and then learn how to create new DNA modifications for quite specific purposes.

... " This may mean that studying different forms of life, a person will be able to create robots that teach themselves and computing systems that set themselves up. Digital implants embedded in living tissue (for example, to enhance brain activity) or living tissue grafted to the digital system. "Perhaps this means the advent of a new era of very fast training," Venter continued. "And this is not the only aspect of human life, which, perhaps, will completely change, thanks to new technologies."

However, this is definitely not the only innovation in the field of 3D-print. Hold on to the chairs, ladies and gentlemen, and meet a machine that can build a completely ready-to-live home in just one and a half weeks - with no unnecessary noise and construction debris. This was recently demonstrated to the world by developers from the Chinese city of Xian. The two-floor house was assembled from the building modules printed on the 3D printer, and then they were fastened together for several hours, like details in the Lego children's game. All modules have already arrived with finished interior decoration, built-in furniture, electrical wiring, and plumbing. In total, it took 6 pieces of 3D modules to build a two-floor house. The entire construction process - from printing to the complete assembly of an apartment house - took only 10 days.

The composition of the material from which the walls of the house were printed is not yet publicized. It is known only that its cost is not very high (1 sq. m. of such housing will cost up to $ 560). In addition, the house has good technical characteristics. It can stand up to 150 years and withstand an earthquake up to 9 points. It has a high thermal insulation: it is not hot in summer and nor cold in winter.

Not stopping at the achieved, during 2014, the Shanghai company WinSun produced the construction of ten 3D printed houses meeting the record 24 hours.

 The baton was picked up by the Arab Emirates. Last year, Dubai opened the first office printed in a 3D printer. A one-floor 800 square meter building was built in just 17 days using a giant 3D printer 6 meters high and a special mixture of concrete, plastic and fiber reinforced gypsum. A huge device with a height of two floors was managed by only one employee (operator). The rest of the construction team of 18 people consisting of builders, electricians and mechanical engineers. The total cost of the work was only $ 140,000 including salary and cost of the material. This is half of the cost for the conventional construction methods. The printed building housed, as previously planned, the Dubai Future Foundation.

"... This is not just a building box, it has fully functional offices and is ready to receive staff," says Mohammed al-Gergavi, one of the UAE ministers. According to the minister, Dubai plans to build 25% of buildings in the emirates using 3D printing by 2030.

When houses are built using the 3D printing method, the technology of the so-called "Contour construction" is often applied. Dr. Bekhrokh Hoshnevis from the University of Southern California is in charge of its development. In its installation, a dispenser stacks a specially prepared mixture layer by layer according to counter set by a computer file.

The peculiarity of this technology is an additional tool of the machine - the manipulator setting supporting structural elements, engineering communications (bridges, floor beams, rafter elements, chimneys, etc.) in the designed position.

The main building material is rapidly hardening concrete, reinforced with steel or polymeric microfiber. More expensive or cheaper types of concrete can be used as depending on the requirements for the performance characteristics of the building. Innovative technology of woven bulk mesh frames can be used as a connecting armature. It is assumed that such frameworks can be linked into a single structure during the construction process. The advantage of this method is a very high construction rate. A house of 150 sq.m can be built by the machine in 24 hours! However, the process is not without drawbacks such as complexity and, in some cases, inability to build buildings with an open layout.

One of the most successful contouring systems is D-Shape developed by the Italian engineer Enrico Dini. The technology of D-Shape is so "advanced" that it allows you to build objects in general without human intervention! In the construction it uses a special technology of converting sand into a mineral substance whose properties, according to some information, exceed Portland cement. This material is so strong that in some cases it does not require reinforcement. In addition, D-Shape allows you to accelerate the construction process up to four times compared with traditional methods.

In 2009, 3 meters high building was already build by the D-Shape system. In 2017, the Dutch architects plan to build an unusual building in the Mobius strip form with the help of contouring technology, as well as the D-Shape system. Plastic obtained in the recycling of waste will be used during the construction. Thus, the company hopes not only to reduce the housing price per square meter, but also contribute to the improving the environmental situation.

No sooner appeared on Earth the technology of 3D construction, than scientists are already looking at the sky. Because in the future the European Space Agency plans to use a technology similar to D-Shape for building space bases on other planets, first of all on our nearest neighbor - the Moon. By the method of contoured layer-by-layer deposition of the material by building 3D-printer it is planned to build residential blocks, warehouses and hangars for future settlers. And the work of the inhabitants of the satellite will certainly be found – at least because scientists discovered an increased content of silver (Ag) in the lunar soil. So prepare shovels for the new Cartagena !

The range of applications of 3D printing has expanded both in depth and in breadth over the past 20 years - from the macro-world to the micro-world. For example, until recently, the main obstacle for individual diagnostic operations in medicine and communications was the size of the batteries of the necessary instruments which often exceeded the dimensions of the instruments themselves. But now a breakthrough is about to happen in this direction - a group of researchers from Harvard and Illinois universities created a lithium-ion battery of a grain of sand size using a 3D printer! (June 17, 2013, the journal Advanced Materials published a scientific paper on this invention).

The components of the battery thinner than the hair had to be printed separately, layer by layer. As a result, there were obtained two objects like a comb forming together an anode and a cathode. They were immersed in the electrolyte solution and a working battery was received.

In the future, I think the implementation of projects, models and just flying fantasies will be limited only by the possibilities of installation, the properties of materials, and also their cost. Already, many installations for 3D printing are able to create objects with the help of several ingredients, and in the future, the range of their universality will only expand. Moreover, objects being copied often have increased accuracy and strength: you can cut with printed scissors, take photos with printed reflex camera etc. This is also facilitated by the growing industry of 3D scanners.

Here are a few bold ideas that have already been embodied by people with imagination.

Food and sweets: The most incredible sweets, cakes and pastries. Note, that candy can be made in two versions - white and colored. You can choose from vanilla, mint, sour apples, cherries and watermelon. This was even shown in the cartoon series "Simpsons". Episode "Futu-drama", 2005, shows a cake featuring Bart and Lisa - a copy of the photograph that Marge made from Bart and Lisa before their graduation evening. As you can see, this humble prophecy was subsequently embodied in reality!

(Source: https://www.adme.ru/vdohnovenie/9-tehnologij-predskazannyh-simpsonami-649505/#image4208205 © AdMe.ru)

Rooms and houses: Designers Mikael Ansmeier and Benjamin Dillenburger printed a 16 m² room from specially prepared fine-grained sand. The room was created in the style of the scenery for the "Alien" movie with a fair share of imagination and without the traditional four corners.

Furniture, fittings and interior items: The company Emerging Objects creates the most incredible furniture in the future style with the help of 3D printing and a drop of artistic fantasy. The bench in the photo is made of a mixture of cement, compressed plastic and concrete and withstands the weight of a small elephant. (© emergingobjects.com)

Snowboards and sports equipment: The coolest snowboards are manufactured by Signal Snowboards from California. Their edges are slightly bent upwards for maneuverability, the design and strength of the product are also high class. The highest score!

Footwear: Designer Janne Kuttänen from the Netherlands printed a collection of women's shoes and posted sketches on the website - they can be downloaded and printed at home in six to seven hours. (© cubify.com)

Musical instruments: Professor Olaf Didel from New Zealand created a series of so-called ODD-guitars. Didel says: "3D printing technology makes possible the production of impossible forms. For example, one of my guitars has the shape of a spider web with spiders crawling inside. " Another man named Scott Summit, who was the first in the world who printed a full-fledged acoustic guitar, says that "it's even better than hand-picked guitars." (© odd.org.nz).

Reflex camera: The author of the idea and technology of producing an SLR camera is Leo Marius. Now everyone who has a 3D printer can download files, print and assemble a camera - in about 15 hours. Materials will cost $ 30 (© leomarius.com)

Prostheses: These eye prostheses were designed by engineers from the University of Manchester and the design studio of Tom Fripp. When such prostheses are made by hand it takes a lot of time and is very expensive - about 3000 pounds. Now, using a 3D printer you can print 150 eye prostheses in 1 hour - and it will cost no more than a hundred dollars.(© frippdesign.co.uk)

Another application of the printer in medicine was found for two-year-old Emma Lavelle, who suffers from congenital muscle atrophy. (© Manufacturing Engineering magazine)

For such people, an exoskeleton has been already developed, but it is too heavy and is not suitable for a small Emma. Therefore, engineer Tarik Rahman and designer

Whitney Sample made for her a lightweight copy of the exoskeleton with a 3D printer. Note that it grows with Emma - all of its parts can be replaced as the girl grows. Now she is 6 years old, and she does everything that her healthy older sister does.

Today, 3D printing installations are considered indispensable in high technology production, and tomorrow they will appear in every home. The production of high-quality clothes, watches and telephones at home is not far off. And then - how the card will lie. Because very soon it will result in the production of metal and paper money, weapons and bank cards. Due to these ideas, some futurologists classify 3D printing installations as global risks or so-called "Black Swans" threatening the existence of human civilization. Naturally, there was a proposal to establish special control over their release. In the uncontrolled process, they say, nothing prevents the group of new "bio-hackers" from starting to punch microorganisms resistant to all modern antibiotics or establish an underground workshop for the production of firearms and devices to undermine bridges and buildings.

For example, more recently, Solid Concepts has demonstrated for the first time to the world what a metal gun printed on a 3D printer can do. The elegant descendant of the famous 1911 (with a phrase from the Declaration of Independence engraved on it) got the name "Reason". The model is printed from metal powder using the technology of large-scale 3D printing of refractory metal parts (Sciaky's EBAM license) looks solid and thorough, and to the great surprise of many people, it justifies its purpose. To date, it has shot more than 5,000 rounds and looks like a new one.

For consolation, I can add that the level of technical knowledge necessary to create such weapons is quite high - so far not everyone can download the desired CAD file from the Internet and start printing their own gun. But what prevents future hackers and terrorists from starting to develop and distribute such software on the Net?

There is one more problem aspect that has a double meaning. It appeared in the US and is called RepRap - a device that reproduces "itself." This topic deserves a separate article - in view of its innovation, but for the modern "everything is sold" industry it poses a certain threat and can significantly affect world events - and leave millions unemployed.

RepRap was founded in 2005 by Dr. Adrian Bowyer, a mechanical engineering teacher at the University of Bath in the UK. On September 13, 2006, the prototype machine 0.2 successfully printed its first own part, which was subsequently used to replace the identical part of the device originally created by another printer.

After 2008, when the term of the Hull's patent expired, the STL open technology and other similar technologies allowed, along with RepRap technology, to earn thousands of companies around the world. After 3D printers learned how to produce details for other 3D printers, they began to fly out like hot cakes. A real 3D boom started: the market grew from 50% to 150% over the year.

In recent years, most companies have moved to a new segment - the production of small and inexpensive "desktop" printers. Such devices are sold, for example, by "AMAZON". Typically, most of the "desktop" 3D printers implement layer-by-layer technology of a molten polymer thread.

The creators of RepRap position their device as a "breakthrough technology" on a par with personal computers or integrated circuits. They do not hide their goals for the speedy distribution of their devices in every home. And then the owners of "everyday demand" products will have to count the losses with tears in their eyes.

Yes, we all seem doomed to Abundance! To this, we are called by the whole Nature, the whole Creation, which, literally, cries about it. But this will be a completely different story. The solution to this potential dilemma lies in a different plane - the field of psychology and human thinking. But that cannot be printed on any printer.

Chapter 3: Not the rocket-type furnace is the energy center of your

house. Of course, we expect the best efficiency from it. And it will not fail!

Since the hunting for the first mammoths, when the wild ancestors of people began to make their cold and uncomfortable stone caves habitable, they began to invent devices for heating the premises and cooking. These items, along with spears, axes and a wheel for the wagon, were of paramount importance for their successful survival. Speech, of course, will go about furnaces, hearths and fireplaces - the energy centers of any house.

The stories of these inventions are rooted in the distant past. The first examples of effective devices for space heating we find in Ancient Greece - a system of heating channels under the floor, which was called "Gippokaust". Later this system was adopted in Ancient Rome, where it was perfected by the famous Roman merchant and engineer Sergij Orata (1st century BC).

On the other side of the globe, in the northern part of China and Korea, similar devices have served for the heating of peasant houses for centuries. In ancient China, they were called "kang", in the north of Korea - "ondol", and the common people called it "Kuduri stove."

The "kang" oven was a wide brick, clay or stone stove, inside of which there was a system of heating channels being also a chimney. Traditionally, the "kang" was covered with bamboo or straw mats on top and was a place for sleeping, children playing, eating food, etc. Such design and arrangement was a distinctive feature of rural houses - fanz, and was extremely effective for that time.

Quite a small amount of firewood was required to keep the heat in the house until the morning. This was even mentioned in the story "The Long White Mountain: or a Journey to Manchuria" by the traveler and writer Sir Henry Evan Murchison (1888).

The only difference between the Korean "ondol" that was used in traditional rural homes from a Chinese analogue was that the system of furnace channels passed under the entire floor of the room, and not just under the couch or part of the room - just like in ancient Greece.

Why did we mention all these remarkable designs? The fact is that they all served as a kind of forerunner to that delightful device for burning fuel, which will be discussed below.

The whole point is that the furnaces were invented by people (and continue to be invented) as long and thoroughly as a bicycle. They carefully selected proven by centuries and introduced modern technical innovations - from one masterpiece to the next. So the project continuing the ancient Chinese and Korean technologies was born. Over time, this invention overgrew with rumours and almost legends. It was reported that this furnace is related to the development of NASA, that it does not give smoke and does not require firewood at all. It was reported about 80-90% efficiency of this furnace, an efficiency comparable only to the furnace of Canadian loggers "Bullerjan", but at a much lower cost. Yes, as they say, "there is no smoke without fire," and today we present a device called a jet-powered stove, or Rocket Stove, the totem object of all permaculture lovers and the object of attention of such a wonderful resource, such as - www.richsoil.com

The history of this remarkable project begins in the 80s of the last century in USA, Oregon, on the premises of the Aprovecho Research Center developing productive, technically simple and inexpensive kitchen ovens for the needs of third world countries.

At that time, the vast majority of human world continued to cook on open fire and constantly faced with two problems - lack of fuel and smoke that eats eyes. It was to correct such shortcomings that the efforts of Larry Winiarski, the technical director in Aprovecho, were directed. Under his leadership, a model of the furnace based on the conventional oil lamp scheme was developed. Larry noticed that when the glass cap is applied the wick burns smoothly, brightly and without soot. Thus, kerosene is consumed very economically, and the efficiency of such a device is very high.

The idea of the Larry Winiarski's oven design is simple to genius. The main part of the structure is a vertical combustion chamber isolated from the external space, so that it keeps the heat. It is the factor that makes the process of pure combustion possible. In addition, the fuel receiver is located in such a way that a secondary air supply is provided below the bottom leading to an even greater removal of the gases obtained from the fuel combustion.

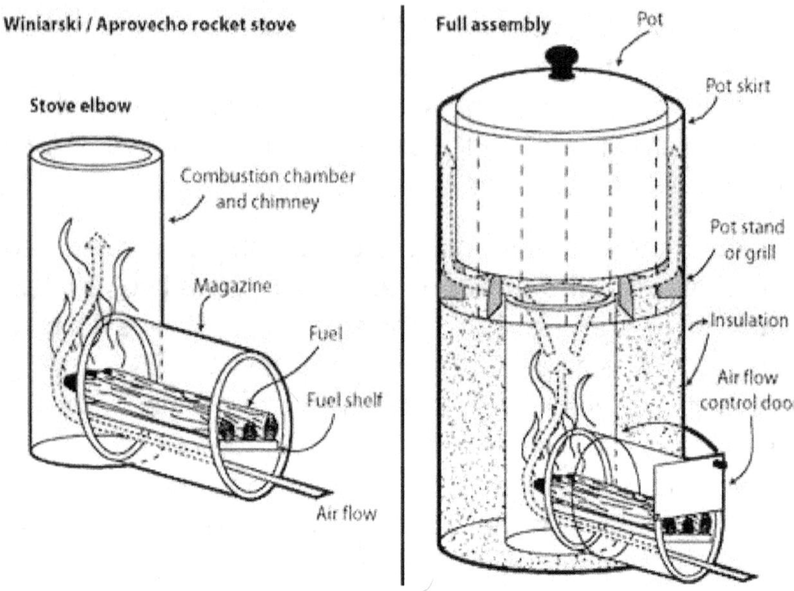

Thus, the engineer Larry Winiarski can safely be considered as the father of all Rocket Stove to this day represented in 12 basic variations, and meeting the main parameters:

- Able to heat your home using 80-90% less wood for this purpose than a conventional oven;
- Exhaust gas - almost pure steam and CO_2 (a little smoke at the beginning);
- Heat from a daily supply of firewood can accumulate for several days;
- 2-3 people can build such an oven in 1-2 days;
- Some people who built them spent less than $ 20;
- This furnace emits less CO_2 than is obtained from burning natural gas in the gas-plate burner;
- Fuel consumption is cheaper than using natural gas. (Source of information - www.richsoil.com)

Larry, together with a group of specialists from Aprovecho and volunteers, starts to travel around the third world countries, demonstrating his invention, arranging training courses and trying to promote the organization of new jobs for entrepreneurs.

Their efforts have been crowned with success, and in a few decades already millions of furnaces in more than 60 countries of the World started puffing up for the joy of their owners. In the meantime, the institute was working on improving the furnace design, as well as to adapt them for various purposes - making pizza, baking bread or heating large rooms. The Institute's developments have been recognized, and in 2006 Larry Winiarski received an award form "Ashden Awards" –an organization that promotes innovation in the energy sector.

Like any good topic worthy of a better continuation, the history of rocket ovens has been further developed by friend of its founding father - his colleague at Aprovecho, engineer Ianto Evans. The field of his interests is very wide - ecology, architecture, permaculture and natural, not harmful to environment construction. Together with Linda Smiley, in 1989 they moved to a new house built by Evans in the "cob" technology. In this building they open a school of unconventional construction from straw, clay and sand called the "North American School of Natural Building," and continue to develop a technology later baptized as "Oregon Cob."

To heat its premises, Ianto aims to modern its colleagues' Rocket Stove. There is an idea to isolate the existing combustion chamber and attach a gravitational fuel receiver to it. A barrel is placed above the vertical combustion chamber for the best heat exchange, and the horizontal channels through which hot air flows from the combustion chamber are cladded around the clay with sand, forming an extension in the form of a bed - just as it is done in the classic "Dutch" or the ancient Chinese "Kan" stove. Such a design is called "accumulative", and it turns out to be very successful - the heated massive couch gradually gave off heat and then also slowly cooled down. Thick and bulk logs were not needed for heating – there were enough chips, brushwood, branches or thin weeds of weedy trees. In the furnace, only the tips of the rods burned, and since the fuel chamber was vertically arranged, gravity forced the firewood to descend gradually until it burned completely. This feature was most likely, spied by Ianto Evans from the Native Americans of the Dakota tribe, who use a similar device in their hearths. Maybe that's why Rocket Stoves are sometimes incorrectly called "Dakota".

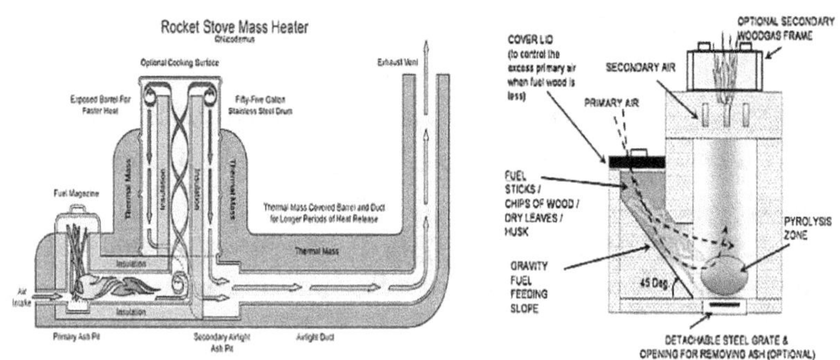

Very high efficiency of such devices seems to be important. In his book on accumulation rocket ovens published in 2006 Ianto reports about 80% efficiency of his device. Basing on such conclusions he compares the amount of firewood he burnt in the winter and the amount of fuel his neighbor used.

It should be noted that the heating the premises with furnace heating is not very popular in the USA today. This does not mean that this topic is not at all relevant to the United States due to not too hot climate on most of the continent. For example, the house of Ianto Evans is located in Oregon near the shores of the Pacific Ocean. The average annual temperature in winter there does not exceed + 1 ºC, which is clearly not enough for a comfortable stay. In short, if something is used from stove equipment for additional heating of apartment houses, it is usually simple metal structures like the Russian "Burzhuyki" or fireplaces devouring an incredible amount of firewood. An additional barrier to the development of classical brick and tile stoves was their very high construction price. Not all Americans were ready to shell out for this order about 15-30 thousand dollars.

A completely different attitude to furnaces for heating houses is in countries with a fairly cold and windy climate, for example, in northern Europe. For them, the issue of efficiency with low fuel consumption is sometimes a matter of life and death, given the relatively high price of electricity and other resources. Therefore, as soon as the news of the outstanding merits of Rocket Stove reached the shores of the North Sea, or rather the Dutchman Peter van den Berg, an engineer in retirement, immediately seized them on his shield and decided to apply them to his advantage. To heat up his house, he already used a duct furnace, made by himself and Finnish type "contraflow". Experiments with the American Ianto Evans' brainchild seemed to him an extremely interesting and important. It was he who first approached this issue from a scientific point of view, deciding to accurately measure all the physical and chemical parameters and indicators in order to improve them.

Armed with knowledge and a professional exhaust gas analyzer, he started measuring. Mostly, he was interested in the productivity of combustion, the level of carbon monoxide CO emission and the coefficient of air excess. Guided by the readings of the analyzer, he made various corrections to the design in order to obtain the desired effect. After numerous attempts in 2011, he managed to make several changes in the classic Evans firebox and invent the so-called J-Tube. To begin with, he arranged the shape of the furnace so that at the end of the combustion chamber a specific turbulence holding the gas flow inside the chamber was created. At the other end of the furnace there were small protuberances that broke the flow of laminar gases and generated turbulence, so that the gases mixed well with the air, and the firewood was completely burned. On the fuel receiver, slots were added, through which additional air was supplied, so that it was possible to reduce the problem with the primary fume intake of the fuel receiver, and also eliminate the unwanted phenomenon with the ignition of the rods to their full length, which sometimes happened during the operation of the furnace. For the device of the combustion chamber, he first used tiles made of the material "vermiculite", so that it was possible to obtain a very fast heat, which contributed to an even more complete combustion of gases. Elements of the construction of the firebox were cast from heat-resistant concrete with a wall thickness of at least 3 cm. Thanks to this "thermos" effect, the temperature in the combustion chamber increased very rapidly, yielding a clean fuel combustion at the outlet after 5 minutes after the match was delivered to the firewood. The average performance was as high as 93%, and the level of carbon monoxide (CO) in the exhaust gas fell very quickly, maintaining an average of 150 ppm.

These are really outstanding qualities, and few furnace designs are capable of repeating similar results. Peter van den Berg's achievements were enthusiastically accepted in the United States and he was offered a ransom of the author's license. Since that time and in the next few years, the J-Tube project will not be available in an open format, and Dragon Heaters bought this license organized the sale and deportation of special postal kits for those who want to burn the combustion chamber in their Rocket Stove in accordance with Peter van den Berg's design. This action caused some concern among the Rocket Stove masters, because before that time all the necessary furnace projects were laid out simply on the Internet open-resource. However, there is nothing to be done, and you will have to wait a certain amount of time, when the license expires, and the J-Tube project can be downloaded.

So, if we already have a device that burns firewood so efficiently, should we think how we can use the full calories it produces? The device of the classical "channel system", or the device of the couch (branch channels, covered with clay with sand) that were used in the ancient Chinese "canes" and in the Ianto Evans constructions is not always good from the point of view of interiors or surrounding materials. In addition, they have a number of design flaws. However, an alternative, more efficient method of maximum heat transfer has been proposed a long time ago. This system is called "chamber" or bell and it is based on the theory of hydraulic motion of gases. It was developed in Russia by Professor Grzhimailo, and later it was developed in the works of Podgornikov and Kuznetsov. In Poland, on this subject there was very much written by the engineer Szrajber, and his developments are worth very carefully look at - certainly by those who are really passionate about Rocket Stove.

The main difference between this system and the channel system is the way in which the stoves use the circulation of hot gases that leave the combustion chamber. Open chambers are used instead of narrow passages just like in a village Russian oven or like covering the fire with a large bell. In this case, the couch can also be arranged in a simpler and more expedient way - unlike the massive and laborious couch from the "cob". The outlet for the exhausted hot gases is placed in the lower part of the furnace, so that already cooled smoke exits out. The main heat remains in the upper part of the furnace, the more time does not cool down. Another advantage of this system is the increased heat exchange capacity - due to the increase of the contact area of hot gases with the internal surface of the furnace in comparison with the system of branch channels. Information about these experiments was hotly debated in online forums devoted to Rocket Stoves. Many people began to experiment and exchange ideas that arose at the intersection and combination of various designs. Among others, an interesting solution was hunt up by a certain Matt Walker, who used barrels sawn half-and-halfand then clad with a clay (half-barrel system).

Do you think this is it? No! Work on improving the Ianto Evans's design continues on this day.

Among the "rocket designers" this furnace is usually associated with a barrel with an open fuel receiver located vertically. Pre-burning fuel is loaded the same way. Along with many advantages, it has a number of shortcomings. For example, the combustion process requires constant presence and supervision - in case of stray coal jumping from the receiver to make a fire. In addition, a small amount of smoke comes out of the receiver, especially at the very beginning of the combustion, when the bulk of the furnace has not heated up sufficiently. Of course, the idea arose to arrange the receiver horizontally, to make it more spacious and to provide a stove door with a "little eye", as it is done, for example in "Bullerjan" - in order to throw wood, close and go quietly to do their own business. It is obvious that all these rationalization proposals should not have been inconsistent with the effectiveness.

This idea was furrowed by the waves of the Internet open resources, and as it happens, one guess born another. Interested in the efforts of his American colleagues, the already familiar engineer from the Netherlands Peter van den Berg, who again took up the development in accordance with the new requirements, is again on the scene.

After numerous tests and analyzes with the help of special equipment, he presented a project of a horizontal combustion chamber called "Batch box". The prototype of this device was originally made of refractory concrete, and the inflow of secondary air into the combustion chamber was increased. The project specified the necessary proportions in which it was required to create such a camera. The tests of the newly baked product showed 92% performance and higher power compared to the previous "J-tube". There were added desired doors with a "little eye" to observe the burning process.

After the publication of these works, samples began to appear like mushrooms after the rain, which already differ little from the classical "tile" furnaces of our time. Professional stoves get seriously interested in Rocket Stove, and their products are increasingly becoming fashionable. It remains only to ponder - whether the baby isn't flushed together with the water in pursuit of modernization and amenities? You can breathe peacefully - the main principle of rocket stoves - "clean burning", laid down at the dawn of "rocket building" by Larry Winiarski remained unchanged, being the key to the popularity of his creation for many decades!

Bringing the fatty line under everything that has already been said, it remains to add that in this story it's still too early to dot the i's and cross the t's. This is due to the fact that not all Rocket Stove models have been scientifically researched to be full certain that there are no better in the world. It is better to listen to the opinion of an independent observer, a good friend of the author of these lines, who has been fond of the Rocket Stove devices for many years.

After he built several models, he was lucky enough to meet with several experts in this field and work with them in pairs, calculating the parameters using the Testo-330 / 2LL exhaust gas analyzer. The measurements showed that Peter van den Berg was right - the average combustion rate was 92-93% and the level of carbon monoxide (CO) was stable at an average level of 450 ppm. After a while, it generally dropped to about 100 ppm. It is interesting to hear what conclusions he made after his research:

- o A well-made professional stove product will have better parameters than a poorly made rocket furnace;
- o A well-made Rocket Stove will have a higher capacity than a stove of average quality from a professional stove maker;
- o A well-made Rocket Stove will run as fast as a well-made classic stove, but it quickly reaches wood burnt with a lower amount of carbon monoxide;
- o The Rocket Stove burning chamber is placed low enough, and sometimes we have to bow before our oven to fill it with firewood;
- o The basic versions of Rocket Stoves are simple enough and you can do them yourself with the help of auxiliary materials. It is, however, necessary to reckon with the possibly short life of such constructions.

But I think he did not say anything about the main advantage. Namely, that there is something magical in our furnaces and fireplaces… The way they flare up, buzz, spreading heat in all directions. Or the taste of potatoes baked on charcoal! You can watch the for hours fire dancing in the logs. So, Rocket Stove, in my opinion is the highest poetry of the stove construction. Quite a bit of wood is needed to make the barrel almost red so it could boil water for tea or for cooking food. Once we tested a Rocket Stove for firing ceramics - in 15 minutes, using a single firewood tab, the calorimeter showed a temperature of 1160 °C! My familiar potters were very impressed.

The sound that the stove emits heating up worth hearing for hours. Probably, because of this, the stove was called so. Among other sounds that emit other hearths, this one was like Mozart among mediocrities ... :)

***Chapter 4**: Lighting and heating: producing free gas. Electricity forever and without payments. Water sorting. Modern technologies leading to savings.*

The world is changing rapidly. The amount of knowledge accumulated through the generations is growing while the number of startups increases smoothly by the hyperbolic curve. It is possible that in the near future those innovations that are now cooling our hearts and ignite our mind will seem insignificant, primitive and ubiquitous – such is the power of this exponential growth.

But this scenario requires more and more resource from the world, for which at all times - from a stick and a fire to space ships - a brutal and non-compromise struggle was conducted - with the conquest of other tribes and the seizure of foreign territories. This struggle happened hot and cold, mental and physical.

The name of this resource is Energy, the elusive and cosmic substance, the equivalent of merit. In ancient Egypt and Mesopotamia, the main "energy carriers" were slaves and domestic animals, whose muscular strength was used.

Add to this plant organics (wood, dried animal droppings, grass) and we get a complete picture of the energy component that existed before the Middle Ages.

Then coal came first in the world's energy balance, and from the first half of the twentieth century (with a very large value of coal remaining), oil and hydropower are beginning to play an increasingly important role. Since the second half of the twentieth century, with the growing role of oil and the diminishing role of wood and coal, there is an increase in the share of natural gas and nuclear energy in it. These are the main milestones in the energy development of mankind.

Now it's time to figure out why this is so important for each of us. If we consider the coefficient of efficiency that is known to everyone from school, the essence of it is to obtain the maximum amount of usefulness for the least amount of Energy. In another case, if the amount of energy is replaced by the amount of money (which is sometimes also called energy substance), then man always strives to acquire a much larger quantity of goods for less money. This is the basis of the economy and the engine of energy-saving technologies, the search for renewable sources and new materials. Since the XX century, new branches of knowledge and sciences have appeared on this subject - "synergetics", "energy design", "ergonomics", etc.

Thus, the effectiveness of any economy, production or individual work is determined, first of all, by three components - the time interval (speed) of implementation, the amount of Energy (resources) that was spent on the process, and the quality of the final product. For example, a pit can be excavated in one day by one excavator or by three workers for seven days, but with the same result.

Reducing the costs taking into account the mental component (human fatigue) is the main issue in the economy. When one talks about the quality and standard of living in a separate state, the defining moment is the volume of energy costs per unit of output (gross national product).

But in this issue, not everything is as simple and unambiguous as it might seem at first glance. For example, for the economy of a particular region, it is easiest to build a thermal power plant that operates on local cheap coal. Such a construction in the basic configuration is relatively inexpensive, but the yield of Energy is small. When attempts are made to modernize it (in order to increase efficiency) and also to connect a number of environmental requirements, the cost of assembling stations increases many times, which ultimately affects the cost of the final product (heat, electricity). Do not forget about the constantly growing number of consumers due to natural population growth. People need to be fed and heated. The development of natural science and the release of oil to the role of global factors provoked the so-called "Green revolution" in agriculture, which, in turn, led to the cultivation of monocultures, the use of herbicides, pesticides, etc. Most of these resources are made from oil, and require huge funds for their production. Economists estimated that for the cultivation of 1 food calorie (taking into account the total energy costs for the entire production cycle), sometimes 15-20 calories of useful energy are expended in the EU and in several US states! So it's no coincidence that in the US and EU the state supports its farmers with huge subsidies. Without these subsidies, produced grain, meat, vegetables, etc. would be uncompetitive at any price.

All this ultimately falls on the shoulders of taxpayers. This creates a kind of "vicious circle" - in order to fill the deficit of energy intensive products, a person spends more and more energy on production and purchase, creating an even greater deficit of resources. The end is not visible.

The only way out of this situation is to use endless, inexhaustible and inexpensive sources to eliminate the energy deficit. Energy production should not harm the environment. It is also diversification, redistribution, refusal of monopolistic and centralized sources of Energy. There should not be any additional links between the Energy produced and the final consumer - each individual house or village must have its own permanent source, be completely autonomous and self-sufficient in terms of energy costs.

After many centuries, the eyes of scientists turned again to the forces of the four Elements - sunlight, water, wind and Earth (energy of decomposition, combustion and photosynthesis). "Intelligent" systems of energy distribution and accumulation are being developed - from places where there is surplus production to deficient places. The next stage of energy independence promises to be the conquest of cold thermonuclear energy - which, perhaps, will fill not only the shortage of electricity on the Earth, but also other elements of the periodic table, including gold and rare-earth metals. And this is not a fairy tale or a bare fiction.

A private American company TriAlpha Energy promises to create the first working commercial thermonuclear reactor already by 2027. This task is extremely difficult. In fact, it is necessary to create something similar to "hidden sun in a box", with the maintenance of the necessary balance for the entire operation of the device.

Since there are still no materials on the Earth that can withstand such high temperatures, the whole thing, as you understand, is to create such a "box". Currently, the company has an installation that allows keeping the plasma heated to 18 million degrees Celsius for about 11.5 milliseconds. The Tri Alpha Energy reactor, unlike most similar machines, should operate on a mixture of deuterium and boron. To start a thermonuclear reaction, it is necessary to heat up this fuel to three billion degrees Celsius. The use of boron, according to Tri Alpha Energy, is preferable to tritium, due to the greater prevalence of the first compared to the second.

 So we have to live in a surprisingly interesting and promising time - on a new spiral of technological revolution. New concepts have emerged - "alternative", "green" and "renewable" energy - the transition from the monopoly of "burning" energy to natural resources (gas, coal, shales, etc.) to cleaner and more accessible sources of Nature. Even the "black blood" of a transport system called "oil" begins to give up its positions, giving way to electric cars or cars that use hydrogen or aluminum powder as fuel (the development of the Israeli company "Alchemy Research").

Today the ideas that some called "insane" yesterday helped to revive entire areas in Austria from the ashes of the economy, or to light and heat up to 60% of the homes in Spanish Seville. More and more powerful players are joining alternative energy, including Ilon Mask with its Powerpack batteries and photocells for roofing and Apple or Google (NASDAQ: GOOG). Even such a whale of the investment world as Warren Buffett prefers to invest in renewable energy technologies without regard to other players. Only, it seems, he has slightly different views on the ways and development of these projects than Ilona Mask.

Of course, we are sometimes far from the capabilities of Warren Buffett. Sometimes, all we have is our hands, a little money and everything that the environment can provide us. The existing plants for obtaining "green energy" often become too expensive. Then the question arises - is it possible to achieve energy independence at a more primitive, everyday level? What can you do with your own hands and spend a little money for this? It turns out that nothing is impossible in this plan - as before, all the forces of Nature are at our disposal. Let's look at these issues in more detail:

- *Use of Sun Energy:*

Every hour our Sun gives the Earth as much Energy as a person uses for a year. The light gives us heat in the form of solar radiation and light (the day's solar spectrum) in the form of elementary particles - photons. These particles are capable of knocking out electrons from some materials, or rather, from their crystal lattices at the level of atoms. The thermal effect of light, collected in one focus, is manifested in the transfer of energy to other conducting media, engendering thermal (Brownian) motion in them. This is widely used in photovoltaic devices, as well as in the production of solar collectors.

Such panels on the roofs of residential buildings have already become a familiar part of the landscape in Western Europe or America. In Germany, for example, owners of such roofs are united in separate communities for the redistribution of energy during rush hours - and receive double benefits from this. Nevertheless, such devices do not lack some drawbacks, for example, the problem of clearing panels from snow and dust, protection from accidental mechanical action, the operation of elements in strong clouds and in the dark at the time has not been finally solved.

To use the energy of the sun, even in the garden house, it should be remembered that the darker surfaces reflect solar radiation weaker than light ones, so they heat up faster on a sunny day. The "warmest" directions are the southern ones. Hence, the roof in dark tones, located on this side, at an angle of 30-45 degrees is able to get the biggest amount of heat.

On the open Internet recourses you can often find ideas for creating household and cheap solar collectors, which can be adapted for heating small rooms. The first method allows the creation of solar panels of empty beer cans in 7 steps:

(https://www.youtube.com/watch?v=KC0I9upweyU).

Another solar thermal module uses a flexible tube from the hood for cooking stoves. According to the resource WarmPod, its assembly can be done in no more than $ 50: (https://www.youtube.com/watch?v=PzXfXTeYdV4)

But, perhaps, the coolest and the most inexpensive way to use sunlight came up to mechanic Alfredo Moser (Alfredo Moser) from Brazil. A genius and simple (as usual) design provides light to thousands of homes in the world's poorest countries where at times even electricity is unavailable. First, water is poured in a 2-liter plastic bottle and a little bleach is added to it to prevent the growth of microorganisms. Then the bottle is pushed out through a small hole made in the roof and the joint is filled with a congealing silicone sealant so that the roof does not leak during the rain.

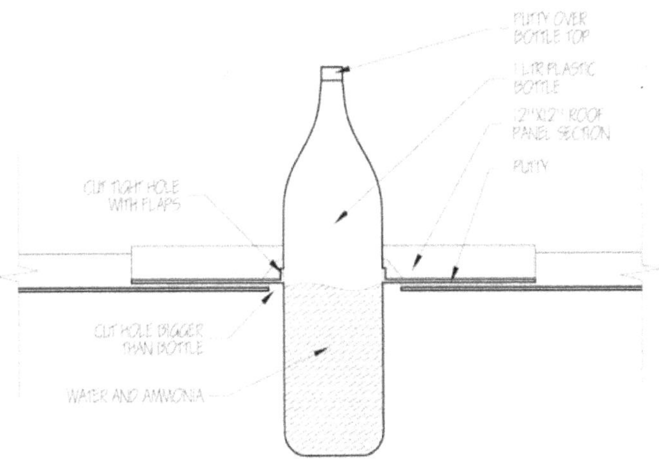

Due to the ray refraction in the water, the bottle effectively dissipates light inside the room. Measurements showed that one 2-liter bottle gives a light flux similar to a 40-60-watt incandescent lamp: (https://www.youtube.com/watch?v=C5XCRg_I4IE)

- o *Use of Water Energy:*

There is an indispensable attribute in the landscape of the countryside - picturesque water wheel that lazily rounds the streams of the current river from the more elevated part of the landscape. Lucky someone who has a house in a rough terrain and not far from a natural pond - it moistens the surrounding air and improves space Feng Shui (unless it is the cause of floods). But the energy of the wheel can be used not necessarily to grind the grain into flour, as it was in the old days. Adjust it to an electric generator and you will receive a source of electricity for the rest of your life. It is possible to act even more cunningly - since the house is usually built at the highest point of the area (for natural drainage and drainage of rainwater from the basement), and an artificial reservoir is created at the lowest point of the area, it is possible to combine a drainage tray with a channel of water flowing from the artificial filter (Swamps) and get a pretty decent stream. Then create a small drop in the height of 1-2 meters for the device of the waterfall and apply the same water wheel with an electric generator. (Why you need an artificial pond with a swamp on the area, I'll talk a little later, when we start the topic of water sorting).

o *Use of Wind Energy:*

If your landscape does not give you fancy full scope, and the terrain is completely flat as a pancake, this option of obtaining free energy will suit you.

Thus, you do not lose anything, because the elements of the winds are as clean and safe as the energy of water. And the wind in some types of terrain is blowing straight constantly - in contrast to the sunlight or water, which can freeze. You save up to 47% of the funds only when connecting to the existing system of windmills in your county. Residents of a small village may chip in for construction of such a structure (the cost of a stationary wind generator is about 15 000 euros together with the installation).

However, it should be taken into account that the wind blows not always strong at the height of the mills. Much more intensive movement of air masses occurs at a much higher altitude - where only birds and kites fly.

A test of a very interesting device was conducted by experts from Loring Commerce Center in Limestone, Maine, USA. Their "hovering wind generators" Airborne Wind Turbine (AWT) is a helium-pumped balloon with a turbine in the middle.

Since helium is much lighter than air, this device rises to the desired altitude and begins to transmit current through the binder to the receiver cable. At the same time, special devices deploy the turbine in the direction of the maximum supply of wind. Such a resemblance to an airship can also be equipped with a module for distributing WiFi - is this not a ready-to-go idea for business in your region?

Using the Internet open resources it is not difficult to make a windmill with your own hands. The main node in the device is the motor. As it, an old but, certainly, serviceable car generator can be used. Such an engine with a wind force of 10 meters per second is capable of producing up to 140 watts. To increase the efficiency of the system, it is necessary to reduce the energy losses of the coil of the generator itself (about 3 amperes). It is best to do this with a new rotor, supplemented with magnets, the number of which directly depends on the number of teeth on the stator. It is recommended to supplement the rotor with a three-phase winding to improve performance. Such a design is able to give from 20 volts already at 250 rpm.

For the manufacture of the mast for the windmill, a steel pipe of 3/4 inch diameter is quite suitable. The only thing necessary to provide a swivel joint and keel, which will allow the windmill to navigate the wind and make the most efficient use of its energy. Blades of a wind generator are simpler and cheaper to make from PVC pipes with a diameter from 110 to 160 millimeters, which are now sold in every hypermarket. Considering that our wind generator is homemade, for better balance and lower vibration, it is reasonable to make 4 blades. In order to make your power supply system truly autonomous, it is necessary to equip it additionally with batteries (preferably gel-based), a charge-discharge controller of batteries, as well as an inverter that will turn the windmill current into a usable household appliance.

However, the wind, as it turns out, can be used not only to generate electricity - but to apply it in an environmental conditioner. This device for the house does not consume electricity at all and consists of recycled materials, any person can make it anywhere in any part of the world. And it works!

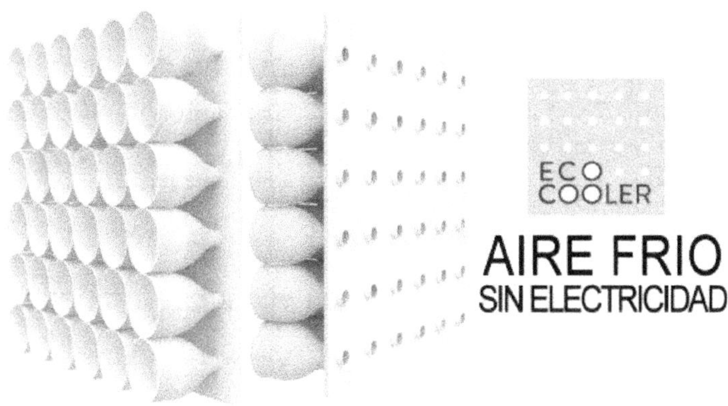

Meet Aire Frio Eco Cooler. It was developed by the Grameen Intel Social Business company, which is engaged in the search for technological solutions accessible to all people. The idea is very simple - try to open your mouth on the diameter of the ping-pong ball and exhale into the palm – you will feel the heat. If you narrow your lips into a tube and blow, you will feel cold. It's all about the difference in pressure, but that's what makes Eco Cooler work. The rest is a matter of technology and, fortunately, very uncomplicated: (https://www.youtube.com/watch?v=KyqaJ1NyJT0)

- o *Energy of biological waste:*

Now we are starting the most delicious part of our research, because we touched on subjects that nobody feels sorry for, and some even puzzle over how to get rid of them. But God, let's not forget, has nothing superfluous, and to force the unnecessary to work for one's own benefit is, I believe, the top of human Genius.

It is known that all biological and production waste can be divided into two main types - organic and inorganic. Our small friends microorganisms (bacteria and algae) are capable of processing both of them - the question is only in terms and side effects. In any case, it will be easier for them to cope with their task if they have to work with smaller particles. In the process of fermenting organic matter at the output, we have:

1. Free gas, similar to methane (with small impurities);

2. Electricity and heat, which can be obtained from the combustion of gas;

3. Excellent organic fertilizer for gardens and fields;

4. Complete disposal of waste.

I believe that now no one needs to agitate for domestic and industrial installations for the biogas production. Such installations should be installed in a new location rather than residential houses - and have a fourfold benefit from their use.

The first experiments on the use of gases, which are obtained as a result of fermentation, originate in the first century BC, but only in the 21st century, scientists interested in it seriously. Today this direction is considered to be one of the most actively developing and demanded sources of energy.

Until recently, there were serious limitations on the used raw materials. All microorganisms involved directly in biogas production could process only prepared biological material with a moisture content of at least 50%. As a result of this restriction, most biogas plants were located on farms and used only agricultural waste.

Modern technology of "dry processing" (developed by the Swiss company Zorgbiogas) allows to significantly expand the list of used raw materials. Domestic waste, solid domestic waste, food waste from restaurants and supermarkets can now serve as fuel.

It should be noted that of all renewable energy sources only biogas and hydroelectric power stations are capable of providing a stable output of energy. Solar cells and windmills provide only 20-40% of the rated capacity and depend on the weather conditions. The weather, no matter what it is, does not effect on biogas stations, while they ensure the disposal of harmful wastes.

Now several pilot projects on the use of Waste Energy are being developed in the world. The palm of the championship for biogas production belongs to China, but in other countries, start-ups in the processes and technologies of recycling grow like mushrooms. Let's try to hold a small hit parade among installations that may interest an ordinary resident of a city or village:

5 place without a doubt can be given to the German social project (B) energy which developed special bags (B-pack) for transporting biogas to hard-to-reach places for the poorest regions of the Earth. The gas-filled bag weighs about 5 kg and provides about 4 hours of operation of the gas burner for cooking.

4 place rightly belongs to biological reactor Biobolsa, which is very similar to No. 5, but also produces fertilizers. In principle, nothing complicated - large, strong membrane bags 15 meters long by 2 meters wide and more than 2 meters high. Their capacity is about 40,000 liters of liquid, and the possibility of processing up to 1 ton of waste per day. There are more compact solutions of 2x2 meters for a small family, they process up to 20 kg of waste. With the help of such biogas plant, one peasant family that keeps 4 pigs can produce enough biogas for use in the kitchen.

3 place I give to the built-up construction of Israeli developers under the name HomeBiogas. This is a small container weighing less than 40 kg., which presents a complete waste recycling system. The capacity of the tank is capable of processing up to 6 liters of organic waste per day or up to 15 liters per day of manure, turning them into fuel for cooking and organic fertilizers. This is an ideal solution for private houses and backyards. The installation uses a simple method of "home" generation of renewable energy. According to the developers, their device can convert one kilogram of food waste to 200 liters of gas - a quantity more than sufficient for cooking for one hour. (https://www.youtube.com/watch?v=xDF8VSRgapl)

2 place must certainly belong to Horse - a machine that converts food waste into electricity and fertilizers. This portable biogas plant completely simulates the processes that occur in the digestive system of a herbivorous animals, such as a horse or a cow. It is able to process up to 25 tons of organic waste, while producing: 20,440 liters of organic fertilizers and 37 MWh of energy, using the strength of bacteria. It can use a wide range of organic waste, from kitchen waste and domestic waste, such as paper, and also generate both liquid fertilizer and energy in the form of biogas and electricity. The system can work autonomously, fully providing itself with all the necessary energy. (https://www.youtube.com/watch?v=bdCgiry3yS8).

But I still would like to give the palm of priority to those simple and inexpensive installations that, thanks to the golden hands of masters from different countries, allow to saving resources and beneficially influence the ecology. For example, the step-by-step instruction of the Indian Antoni Raj (http://www.instructables.com/id/Constructing-a-Medium-Sized-Biogas-Plant-Using-Kit/) consists of 10 simple operations on the use of weeds. Video materials on the assembly, installation and operation of such devices are freely available. All of them, as a rule, consist of 4 main nodes:

Biological reactor for receiving the prepared substrate (this means - thoroughly crushed). For better fermentation and activation of the fermentation processes, this container should be heated up to 38-40 * C (it is possible to get the energy from burning some of the biogas obtained), mix the substrate thoroughly during the bioreactor operation, and add water if necessary. Also the possibility to remove spent substrate, which is an excellent organic fertilizer, should be foreseen.

An improvised gasholder (a 200-liter tin can fit), equipped with a device for measuring gas pressure.

An electric compressor for supplying gas to the cylinder, ready for use in a gas burner.

Now when we have decided on the economy and rational use of the three communications - heat, gas and electricity, it's time to think about the smart water flow. This theme seems to me the most important, because a person is 70% of it - it turns out that this is our human Nature. At the present time, many solutions are proposed for both the most   arid   regions (https://www.youtube.com/watch?v=pjjw21JPD5c) and for the reuse of water in regions with sufficient content of this resource.

The most interesting to me are ideas on water extracting by condensing atmospheric moisture at the dew point in industrial and domestic installations using, as in the video: (https://www.youtube.com/watch?v=GvXP-hxs9eA). Such water is suitable for drinking and even has medicinal properties (if, of course, it is obtained in ecologically clean regions).

In most places of human settlements there is no water deficit, as it was peculiar to settle near rich sources and with sufficient amount of precipitation. However, we should not forget that the existing amount of fresh water makes up only 1-2% of the total water balance of the planet. An increasing number of it is consumed by modern industry. For example, for the extraction of oil by fracturing the formation, thousands of cubic meters of purified drinking water are pumped into the wells, which disappears irrevocably. Does not this explain the fact that the cost of clean water is constantly increasing?

Of course, the country house offers many more options for the rational use of water. However, some solutions are suitable for the city:

First, you should divide the entire amount of consumed moisture into 2 main types - technical and drinking. Technical water, free of coarse mechanical impurities, may be useful for cleaning, washing, showering, in the toilet, washing dishes, etc., unlike drinking, which is necessary for cooking or other delicate procedures. Technical water is easy to prepare from natural sources or by collecting atmospheric precipitation. For these purposes it is very useful to construct an artificial reservoir in the lowest place of relief - then it can be used both in the house (by using a drainage submersible pump) and for watering plants in the garden. The supplier of such water is, first of all, the drainage system of our house, or more simply, the roof with tides.

After collecting technical water, the question of how to clean it arises. Simple disposal of coarse mechanical impurities will give a layer of 20-30 cm of washed quartz sand (even better - a mineral "zeolite"). Adding layers of absorbent material (for example, non-woven polypropylene linen - lutrasil) and a layer of activated angle (or burnt coal of shallow fraction and only hardwoods). Passed through successively laid layers of these ingredients, water of any quality becomes suitable for drinking. Adding natural stones to the drinking water cleans it from harmful chemical compounds. Pieces of silver dropped into the water also contribute to purification. The washing of wounds with such water promotes their rapid healing.

The waste water can be recycled. For example, the brilliant American technologist and futurist Jacques Fresco in his film "Projected Future" shares for free the project on combining the shower with the toilet tank. In any case, it should never be thrown away at once, but thought about the possibility of including water in a closed cycle of use.

Such an opportunity is provided, for example, by creating an artificial swamp near your pond. These structures, which are simple to make and care, take on themselves the tasks of revitalizing and cleaning the waste water, preventing the source from drying out. Such an ingenious idea in its simplicity came in mind in 1953 to an enlightened woman named Käthe Seidel from the Max

Planck Institute in Germany. Since then, the principle of an artificial bog remains unchanged - it is a specially designed wetland ecosystem simulating natural patterns in which, due to a combination of physical, chemical and biological processes, the water coming from there is purified from organic and inorganic impurities in such a way that the water coming out from there corresponds to necessary parameters.

What is an artificial swamp? Typically, this is a pool, filled with biologically active substrate (gravel, sand, etc.), through which the water passes while purified. Water- or moisture-loving plants usually grow on the substrate, performing an important function of maintaining the necessary conditions in the ecosystem.

Nevertheless, the main role in the process of water purification is played not so much by plants as by different microorganisms living in the substrate and by the root part of plants. Water can flow completely under the surface of the substrate (closed swamps), and can permanently or periodically cover its surface and look like a pond (open swamps). Each of these types has its advantages and disadvantages. In practice, due to its compactness and efficiency, closed swamps with vertical water currents have been used more and more recently. Previously, for effective work, large areas, covered by a quagmire, were required. In modern swamps, designed according to the "latest word of science and technology", the area necessary for filtration was reduced to 1-2 square meters per conditional resident of the house, which positively affects the cost of the structure. A simple and small swamp with horizontal water flow for purifying gray water (in which there is no water from toilets) can be made by yourself. To do this, you need to dig an elongated groove in a 50-60 cm deep land with a slight incline in one direction, send the bottom and sides waterproof film, lay a drainage perforated pipe in a deeper part, and fill a few cubes of small gravel. Then dig around somewhere near the cattail and reeds and transplant it into the gravel every 50 cm. From the opposite pipe directly to the surface is fed with dirty water (for example, from the shower or washing machine) - so the process of processing is carried out. However, if the task is to build a full-fledged and effective filter for wastewater treatment, it is definitely worthwhile to involve environmental engineers with the necessary qualifications or familiar with all the latest developments in this field.Artificial swamps do not require the cost of their maintenance or special care. At the same time, they significantly revitalize the surrounding landscape and help to maintain water balance. A dozen of mosquitoes or croaking frogs in the evenings do not contribute worsening the overall quality of life, don't it? ☺

End of the first part

PART II:

«CREATION AND SUCCESS »

In the Part 2 of the "Guide on successful Ideas: ..." you will find a continuation of a series of books under the common title "Own Land" and together we will continue to plunge into the amazing world of small and great opportunities.

It is necessary to determine the basic algorithm of our research - in what direction we suggest you to dig and how deep. The understanding of human happiness is a rather abstractive subject of human sciences. On these issues, modern institutions of knowledge sometimes send us unnoticed to the sections of scientific Pedagogy, which my father somehow called "pseudo-

science." Scientists often reflect on the improvement of the nature of Man, work on "Eugenics" and offer success strategies that are suitable for the person best - but not specifically for you. Is this the only thing? In this attempt to blink our eyes they are superior to all the ancient sophists since the time of Platon, but they keep silent about one very important aspect.

This factor is called "the nature of Man", which hardly needs improvement. And Man and any other creation come to the Earth completely perfect, at the time and with the Tao, and man is not able to improve something in a living creature, which our Creator make so well. In other words, not morality, politics or studies make a person better, but the conditions for life and the cleanliness of the environment in which he lives. You do not need to be a wizard from Oz ("The Wonderful Wizard of Oz") to understand this. Another thing is that, when these wonderful opportunities come, your eyes should be open. Books from the series "Own Land" are like a Pandora's box but on the contrary. Flowers of Success usually grow normally at the crossroads of Desire and Opportunity. We only offer chances to disrupt them.

Chapter 5: Work in the garden: what do you need to do, how can you work as little as possible with the results just pleasing? Bonus trek: Ode to the Cannabis sativa.

I would like to begin this chapter with something good, but I will have to start with a big and bitter pill.

The fact is that by 2050 the world is likely to be hungry. This is the forecast of the UN Food and Agriculture Organization. Experts see the reasons for the lack of food in the large-scale degradation of agriculture, the reduction of the fertile soil layer, water shortage, climate change, and overpopulation. The only way out of this is to increase food production by 70% but without prejudice to the environment. How do you like that?

In the "before perestroika" Russia, this expression was popular - "the battle for the harvest". As time has shown, losses in such a war were almost not considered, and all the weapons – light and heavy, chemical and biological – went into the "battle". Tons of pesticides, which poisoned all living things including birds and fish, were poured on the plants. The work of diesel engines consumed whole rivers of poor-quality fuel, and in the fields there often remained skeletons of tracks deceased in this battle. But this war is not won until now.

The reason is that it was conducted with nature and against nature, against that mother or the substance that gave birth to us. Now, please note that between our custom to conduct business and the balance of phenomena that we observe in nature there was always existed a striking difference, please agree. It turns out that this is definitely the world of "everything is not thank God" people, and we have whole bunch of problems, of which the most important is the deficit. In nature, its centuries-old established ecological links, there were never any problems as such (in the usual human sense), and its whole essence is directed towards Abundance and self-sufficiency - which it successfully achieved. It always felt great - with or without a human.

However, there were "renegades" who did not submit to "His Majesty Gross", did not lie down in the "battle for the harvest" and did not want to suck out everything that is possible from Nature to the last drop of blood. They learned from Nature, tried to make friends with it and find reasonable approaches. These "white crows" or "nerds" studied organic farming, applied the basics of permaculture in their farms and creatively developed them. But their undoubted success is someone's lack of profit. This is, first of all, a blow to the sacred cow of the system, in whose veins black blood called "OIL" flows.

All modern farming methods are sharpened precisely for oil. After the Second World War, the Krupp conveyors, which were making tanks, after a small alteration, went to the production of tractors. To replace heavy manual labor, new types of technology were invented, which consumed only oil. Most types of plant protection products are made from oil. The film for greenhouses, containers, clothing, mittens, appliances – thousands of titles. And how did our ancestors do without all this?

Another blow of the system fell on seeds and plant varieties. Ten years ago, the transnational corporation Monsanto (USA) controlled almost a quarter (23%) of the world market for its own seeds. (* ETC Group report "Who Owns Nature?" November 12, 2008). It leads the world's top three seed producers (Monsanto, DuPont, Syngenta) and, in fact, has deprived the privilege of seed production from their farmers due to unbearable competition and bureaucracy.

In the free sale more and more often you may find packaged seeds with the mark "F1". What does this mean? This is a modified plant hybrid or, more simply, a mutilated genetically diverse plant. Its distinctive feature is the ability not to tie seeds with a mother plant to meet new qualities. All this is done to ensure that the next year you again buy a similar sachet of seeds from the Monsanto corporation.

But this is not the saddest thing. The saddest thing is the lack of culture and knowledge, the global isolation of modern human from the delicate energy and knowledge of the Earth. This is especially true for residents of large cities. Many farmers are associated with something basest and not prestigious, difficult and tedious work of working cattle.

And very few people know that it is possible to work on Earth cheerfully and ingeniously, enjoying the results of the work being done. But for this there are several indispensable conditions:

o   First, work on the ground must be made meaningfully and scientifically (not by intuition and not in accordance with the tradition established in your region) and on time;

o   Secondly, it is necessary to observe not only your own interests but also take into account the needs of others and of Nature as a whole;

o   The third condition is to exchange the accumulated experience and knowledge, as well as teach it to children. Perhaps, all this can be found in any manual for achieving Success, for example, Lafayette Ronald Hubbard.

Now, before embarking on the disclosure of the topic of intelligent agriculture, it is necessary to determine - why does it still give birth? What is the basis of soil fertility? How can you spoil the soil, make it lifeless, and how can you improve it?

The soil consists of two types of chemical matter - organic and inorganic. Plants use both, but they assimilate nutrients for their root system only in a special chelate form - therefore, fresh water is an indispensable attribute in fertility. The other obligatory links are all living and dead organisms, plants and animals - from the largest to the invisible to the eye. They "process" the organic matter and produce "food" for plants. Without the third component - mineral composition (sand, clay, etc.), plants can do well. This composition is, in the main, only a support - therefore, plants can be grown only by pollinating the aqueous nutrient solution of its roots.

For a long time scientists could not understand what is the main thing for increasing soil fertility. At the same time, the people's experience, without delving into the subtleties of the processes, achieved good results on its sites. Trying to understand this, a Japanese microbiologist, Dr. Teruo Higa realized the leading role of microorganisms and for the first time applied the microbiological complexes when growing plants. He realized that the whole essence of soil improvement consists in the process of feeding living creatures that live in a huge quantity in the uppermost layer of it (just as we observe it in the ocean). If these creatures do not lack food (organic), then they feed plants too. If they are hungry - the plant suffers as well. This plays a major role in determining the amount and rate of application of organic materials for harvesting. There is a very simple principle of calculation - to add as much organic material as you have harvested the crop by weight (because in nature it is assumed that the whole crop will fall to the ground, and not go to your table).

So, all soils can be formally divided into "living" - more fertile and "dead" (empty) - requiring mineral top dressing. All modern agriculture is carried out, basically, on dead soil. "Living" soil, unlike the "dead" soil, has a pronounced granular structure, it looks shiny and moist, full of various small inhabitants (primarily earthworms), and has a pleasant smell of forest litter. The spade enters it without much effort; It is light and airy. This is due to the so-called "gaps" – structured voids containing air. They play a dual role - first, they contribute to a better air exchange, which is very important for the roots. Secondly, on their walls from the inside, moisture forms at the "dew point" - therefore, such soil suffers less from a lack of moisture. It should be remembered that living soil can be easily and quickly made dead - if you do not return to it what you take from it every year. At the same time, the process of turning dead soil into a living one is much more complicated and requires much more effort. The simplest and the best thing that can be recommended in this case is to leave the site for 2-3 years to grow weeds, regularly mowing them and leaving the remains in place.

Any deep loosening of the soil (especially deep plowing with a turn of the seam) breaks its structure, destroys the soil microflora and weakly fights weeds - although it is for this, in essence, intended. The introduction of monocultures contributes to the development of diseases and pests, which in combination leads to a decrease in yield. For increasing yields, they are fighting with the help of biotechnologies and by developing new areas for plowing (giving preference to the latter). Which, of course, cannot go on indefinitely – because the Earth is not rubbery and is not for human use only.

Another important problem is the increase in the pH of the soil medium (acidity). This is not only a direct consequence of the "greenhouse effect" but also the inefficient use of mineral fertilizers. A huge amount of carbon dioxide and other heavy compounds that are contained in automobile exhaust, the green biomass of the planet cannot reprocess - some of them are bound in the form of atmospheric precipitation into the soil and oceans causing massive death of corals on the shallows and disrupting the overall balance of the ecosystem.

Biological technologies do not stand still, and the transfer of the amount of accumulated experience and knowledge into a new quality is just around the corner. The solutions are offered the most ambiguous - from growing a mushroom oyster mug on used baby diapers to home installations for the production of edible larvae rich in animal protein. Another option for urban conditions involves the construction of vertical buildings – farms. Similar structures are being built, for example, by the Swedish-American company Plantagon International. Their first architectural project was named Plantagon Greenhouse Building B1, and now the first complex is being built in the Swedish city of Linkoping. The vertical farm will be a transparent ball with a height of 17-storey house. Vegetables will be grown in trays, located along a giant spiral. Seeds and tubers will be delivered to the top of the special lifts, and as they mature, they will descend the automatic conveyor down to the first floor where harvesting will take place. In addition, high-rise farms will probably be equipped with a system for processing organic waste into biogas.

Scientists also refer to other sources for obtaining products of the future – marine fish farms, hydroponics, soybeans, algae, the cultivation of edible fungi on forest waste, etc.

But in terms of cost and efficiency, all these methods do not go to any comparison with the advantages that give what has been known for thousands of years and so is not fully used - namely, organic farming.

This form of use offers the greatest biological diversity, the least damage to the environment, high yields, gradual release from diseases and pests, and most importantly - the lowest cost of final products due to lower energy costs. It can be conducted both at the macro level (eco-farm) and micro level (homestead land). If you are the happy owner of the latter, then consider that you are lucky - your family will not be hungry for sure. Maybe you have to do a little to reduce the area of the lawn, but you will save on gasoline for its cutting ☺

So, I propose to go back to the beginning of the chapter and draw a perspective of land management fun and interesting, as promised. All operations on earth are carried out in stages - just as a person dresses in the morning. I believe that if a man gets up from his bed, pulls his panties over his jeans, he, at least, is a great original.

> 1. Suppose you have a piece of land that is well or partially illuminated, with access to water, but completely "bare" (without large vegetation). It should be determined what exactly you want from it. For example, you want to eat fresh fruits and vegetables for most of the year, children need space for games, and old people like to retire in a shady corner of the garden. In accordance with this, the plan of your site is drawn - taking into account the interests of everyone. It should be borne in mind that garden

beds are best placed in the light penumbra of taller trees and shrubs to reduce transpiration in the direction of the rows from north to south - facilitating the work of insect pollinators. The project of the site can be reproduced for the beginning on millimeter paper at a scale of 1/100 (1 cm on the plan corresponds to 1 meter on the ground), measuring the preliminary plot with a wooden compass (step equal to 1 meter), which in Ukraine is called a "goat". To measure the value of the angles of the site, a "leveler" or an ordinary compass is used.

2. Having studied the norms of consumption of vegetables and fruits for each member of the family on the Internet, knowing the approximate yields of each crop, the optimal number of trees, shrubs and areas under the beds is calculated (with a normal margin in case of possible losses). Vegetable ridges can be made of any length, but the width must be defined - this is the length of your hand, multiplied by two.

3. Now is the time to look around and think - what can all this be made of without resorting to significant expenses? The material for conducting organic farming is, most often, right under your feet. If you are, of course, a man of resource.

When creating the most productive for small areas of elevated ridges (another name - Jacob R. Mittleider's narrow ridges) you will need material for the walls of the necessary box. Everything is suitable - old boards, logs, sheet slate, brick, rubble stone (it all depends on whether the building is permanent or temporary). The height of the walls is up to 25 cm for plants with powerful roots (daikon, potatoes), and less for other crops (from 16 cm). As you can see, all this depends on the size of the root. If you are applying boards, then on the inside it's good to provide insulation from moisture.

4. Now, when the boxes are ready, it is necessary to fill it with a nutrient substrate (leaving about 5 cm from the top of the walls unoccupied). On the turf (mown weed) or lawn is put on top of one coat of coarse cardboard, or a couple of layers of any paper trying not to leave any loopholes for weeds. A nutrient substrate is poured from above. The prepared substrate is any organic matter (stems and leaves of weeds without flowers and rhizomes, waste of cultivated plants, straw, old rags, paper, food residues, etc., etc. - in short, everything that is capable of decomposing into priming). A much greater effect is brought about by the preliminary shredding of organic materials in special devices - domestic or industrial shredder for feed or other garden waste, or in any other device that can grind and mix your organic materials.

5. After the main "cultural layer" has been created, it must be carefully pierced with a special solution. This solution is an aqueous dispersion of effective microorganisms - we will dwell on its production in detail.

Effective microorganisms (abbreviated - EM) is a set of living components of the soil environment decomposing the organic matter and working on soil fertility. It can be obtained in everyday conditions by simple operations (look on the Internet) and can be simply bought in the garden center in the finished form. In the sale it most often comes as a special concentrate - the bacteria contained in it need to be awakened and multiplied for more successful work. Concentrate is a yellow-brown liquid with a pleasant smell of yogurt and acidity of not more than 3.5 pH. If the drug has a bad smell and acidity above 4.0 pH, then it is better not to use it – probably, it is expired. To prepare the working solution, add 30 ml of the boiled water without chlorine (preferably the purified rainwater) cooled to 20-35 °C. Concentrate and 3 tablespoons of treacle (jam, artificial honey, in extreme cases - sugar). The solution is well mixed and kept in a glass container without access to air, in a dark and warm place for at least a week. On the readiness of the drug says a slightly sour and pleasant smell of freshly cut hay.

Such a working composition is used in a concentration of 1: 1000 (for 10 liters of warm, clean water without chlorine, 1 tablespoon of the drug is added). When growing seedlings or flowers in pots, a solution of 1: 2000 is used, i.e. The drug is used in 2 times less. After the preparation of the working solution, it must be used as soon as possible - after 3 days it will no longer be suitable.

So, go back to point number 5 and carefully spill our main culture layer from the watering can until it gets wet from the top and bottom. Now, some advisers recommend waking up pieces of broken glass from the top to protect them from mice *. (* The author did not apply this method and therefore does not guarantee his effectiveness).

6. It remains only to fill the upper nutrient layer (EM compost) with a layer of not less than 5 cm for the primary rooting of the seeds or, more preferably, the finished plant seedling. But in order to describe how to properly prepare compost, also requires a small lyrical digression.

There are 2 types of preparation of EM-compost: aerobic (prepared with a free supply of air) and anaerobic (prepared with restriction of airflow). Both species have their advantages and disadvantages. The first type of compost can be produced in a larger volume (it is not necessary to dig a pit for its preparation) plus it has a shorter fermentation period. But the temperature in the process sometimes increases significantly, which negatively affects its nutritional value.

The second type of preparation does not require temperature control, and the compost retains all the nutritional value of the organics. However, because of its structure, it is more difficult to seal it in the soil.

Effective microorganisms are able to process any type of organics. However, there is one rule - the more diverse are the components of the EM compost and the more they are crushed and mixed, the better for its quality. It is very important to add porous materials (straw, grass, sawdust, fallen leaves), crushed brown coal and turf ground at the rate of 10 kg per 100 kg of compost. In a garden watering can with 10 liters of water, add a EM preparation in an amount of 100 ml and 100 ml. (Gram) of molasses or a thick sugar syrup. Thoroughly spill from the watering cans layer by layer. As a result, the moisture content of the compost should be about 40% * (* wet, but the water does not drip from it - author's comment)

For anaerobic process it is more convenient to ferment fermentation in a pit 0.5 m deep. Compost must be compacted, covered with film and sprinkled with earth. After 2 weeks it will be completely ready.

For an "open" method, the organics preliminarily treated with an EM preparation are best collected in a mound about 1 meter in height and 2.5 meters in diameter at the base. At the bottom of the structure it is necessary to radially lay the poles, and from above lay large branches. With this method, it is desirable to increase the humidity of the compost to 60%. For better air access, the ends of the poles are raised periodically, shaking the heap.

Usually the process of fermentation with the "open" method takes about 1.5 - 2 months. But most of the time, a large amount of freshly mown grass and other greenery gets into the compost and it starts to "burn" in the sun. At the same time, the temperature of the mass is significantly increased (up to 60-70 * C), and the work of the EM-drug is actually stopped. This is a very useful phenomenon, because along with the temperature rise, pathogens, helminth eggs, pest larvae and weed seeds are killed. But to save the drug, it is recommended to start compost wetting with plain and warm water, and finish using the formulation, the recipe of which is given above (a week after overheating). The mass of bacteria in such compost begins to grow vigorously only if a small amount of ash or complex mineral fertilizers is added and the temperature of the mass does not rise above 40 * C. Otherwise, the enzyme process

Effective watering: Once again, a well-prepared substrate suffers less from a lack of moisture. But the weather at the moment is a very capricious thing, and plants sometimes need moisture very much, especially during the ripening period. The simplest, but at the same time the most labor-consuming solution to this problem is watering from the garden watering can. But even here there are several subtleties - the water should be kept at least 24 hours and heated to 20-30 * C. If you collect rainwater, then you can skip these conventions - it better wets soil particles. Watering, in order to save water, is best to be done either in the morning hours before sunrise, or in the evening - after sun sets.

A more reasonable solution is watering from natural or artificial water bodies, rivers, canals and streams. If you have permanent source of water nearby, consider that you are lucky. We construct small wooden box near the shore and place a drainage submersible pump in it - the problem with watering is solved. Or you create, if possible, an artificial pond (water pond) at the lowest point of your area, collect snow and rainwater from where and pump it by means of the same drainage-submersible pump (see chapter 4).

For the most "smart lazy people" there are three other ways, also invented by very intelligent people. The first method consists in pulling a thin polyethylene mesh with cells not larger than 1 per 1 cm above the ridge. In the morning and in the evening a large amount of moisture in the form of dew accumulates on it. It remains only to gently shake this mesh with a broom or a hand and water will fall into the soil.

The second method consists in dropping small jugs with a narrow neck (about 3-4 liters) at a distance of 0.5-1 m. It is very important that these jugs are made only of natural clay without any coatings - otherwise you will not achieve the desired effect. Why is this necessary? Pour in a container of natural clay cold water on a hot day, and immediately see how its walls begin to "sweat". This phenomenon is called "osmosis", and water penetrates through the walls of the vessel precisely due to it. Therefore, if you pour water into the buried pots, after a while the roots of the plants begin to suck the water, enveloping the roots of the whole jug. Such irrigation earthenware jugs are used, for example, on a small family farm Urban HomeStead in California, where with 400 square meters collect 3 tons of vegetables. According to the farmers themselves, they are 80% more efficient than drip irrigation. (https://www.youtube.com/watch?v=KGxqShoGKFl).

I will not argue with this, but drip irrigation systems remains one of the smartest and easiest ways to water plants effectively today. Yet it was invented by the Israelis - people who built the man-made oasis in the middle of the desert. This method is suitable mainly for those who are very fond of their garden - for installation and start-up of drip irrigation systems, most likely, it will require the participation of specialists and the greatest material costs from all the above methods. But the effectiveness of this method of watering is beyond praise.

The reader, of course, does not interfere with inventing his own way of rational irrigation. At the same time one important principle must be observed - moisture must flow directly into the root zone of plants, and not to some other place. Otherwise, watering becomes an occupation meaningless and even harmful, leading to a loss of time and precious resources.

Effective fertilizing and removal of weeds. Let's try to sort everything out. Currently, there are three main types of fertilizers -

a) *Mineral fertilizers*: In enlightened Europe, up to 1000 kg of mineral fertilizers per hectare are already introduced. This explains the increasing cost of production and the increase in state subsidies for it. The reason for using these fertilizers is very simple: plants really need affordable, dissolved elements. There are a lot of them in the soil. In the "chernozem" of Ukraine, for example - up to 100 tons / hectare! But they are all packed in the soil absorbing complex (SAC). Without trying to free them, that is, to create fertility, farmers just pour mineral salts on top. And they receive a crop increase. Expensive and harmful - but no need to think!

b) *Undecomposed organics*: The return of organic substances is a necessary and sufficient condition for sustainable agriculture on this planet. For millions of years, all natural ecosystems have demonstrated: they are absolutely stable and self-sufficient. The application of 1 ton of organic material gives an increase in 3 tons of harvest biomass, that is, it increases the conservation of solar energy by half. Accordingly, energy costs for agrotechnics are half reduced, and the profitability of the working farm doubles. Now we return to the soil 20-30% of plant biomass - mostly roots and other residues. This is too little. To maintain fertility, you need to return the soil all manure, and feces, and all plant waste. For a grain crop of 25 pounds / hectare, plants need about 100 kg of macro- and microelements, and about 1000 kg of dry organics to produce carbon dioxide and microbial service.

Farmers are not very fond of dealing with organic fertilizers - they are often too heavy and not convenient for application, have a very unpleasant smell. Another thing is if they are prepared on special devices in a form convenient for transportation and in dry condition - in the form of granules, pellets, etc. They have an optimal composition of mineral elements and contain a maximum of fresh organic energy. Such fertilizers already exist and they are called –

c) *Organic and mineral fertilizers:*

- o "Delaplant" (DELA, Germany) - a mixture of manure and straw particles is partially composted, then treated with activator and fertilizer, dried and granulated. Organic and mineral fertilizers (OMF) are obtained. In the process, up to 30% of organic substances are lost. The equipment cost about 3 million old deutsche marks, the energy costs are quite high, and the activator is supplied only by the firm;

- o "Harmony" (USA) - obtaining OMF by drying manure, mixing with fertilizers and special concentrate. The mixture is subjected to additional drying and granulation. Fertilizer is very valuable, but one third of the organic is lost during the preparation process, the equipment is expensive, and drying in drums for drying requires up to 500 kg of fuel to remove every ton of moisture;

- o Granulated organic fertilizers (GOF) of Swedish and Dutch production are a product of anaerobic microbial fermentation of manure. Installations are just as expensive. Loss of organic in the manufacturing process - more than 30%.

Much cheaper and more successful are russian development:

- o BAMIL, OMUG and PUDRET - GOF from pig, cow and avian manure, developed in the scientific research institute of agriculture by professor I.A. Arhipchenko. The scientist applied simple, mixed way of fermenting raw materials with the possible addition of nutrient components. The product turned out to be more valuable and biologically active than European analogues, and much cheaper. Loss of organic matter is about 1/3, and dryers consume a lot of energy.

Obviously, the most cost-effective technology for obtaining OMF for today is the development of the Bashkir Engineering Center for Organic Processing, introduced at the initiative of the leading specialist O.V. Tarkhanova.

The principle of preparation of these OMFs is completely different from that of granulated organic fertilizers (GOF). Very rude, it looks like this - manure is sterilized by formalin. At the same time, its organic matter is preserved. Then, under certain conditions, carbamide is added. The formed condensation products are superior to conventional nitrogen fertilizers: they act very slowly, reduce nitrogen losses, release CO_2 and stimulate the soil microflora. The processed substrate is dried quickly in a "boiling bed" installation and granulated. At the same time, drying method, developed by the authors, is more economical than the traditional ones - and this is the decisive plus of technology. To receive a ton of fertilizer, only 100 kg of fuel and 100 kW of energy are wasted. New OMFs have been studied and tested for more than ten years. Field tests showed a lot of advantages of these fertilizers. Falling into the soil, OMF is quickly absorbed by bacteria and becomes a source of dynamic fertility.

Of course, all mentioned types and methods of production are interesting, rather to owners of large farms and farmers. For other users, all the necessary "feeding" of plants is already laid in narrow ridges. For prevention and as an additive, you can recommend a very simple way - watering ridges not with simple water, but infused with herbs and weeds. To do this, of course, they must first be laid on the bottom of a large container and crushed with a lid cut from a metal mesh, or pour a layer of coarse-grained sand on top. In this water for irrigation it is good to add 1-2 caps of an aqueous solution of complex mineral fertilizer (obligatory elements - nitrogen, phosphorus, potassium).

To combat weeds, very old and time-tested methods are used - mulching and weeding. Mulching cuts weed seeds from the light, and if they appear on the surface, it is very easy to remove by simple pulling. For greater efficiency of the process, after every weeding, it is recommended to update the layer of mulch and make additional watering.

It is necessary to think about excluding the entry of seeds, flowers and rhizomes of weed plants into nutrient substrates of narrow ridges. If possible, separate everything from the weeds that can shoot. The remains of weed plants are either burned, or soaked for several weeks to obtain a nutrient infusion for irrigation.

If the ubiquitous weeds still penetrated your vegetable patches, it is not necessary to mess with them in a bowing post every day. For these purposes the Russians, for example, have a special tool called the "flat cutter" Fokin. It is illustrated in the picture, and fulfills the following functions:

a.   Pinpointing the weeds;

b.   Loosening the top layer of the soil;

c.   Making wells for seedlings;

d.   Raking the plant remains;

e.   Doing small furrows and soil the roots;

f.   Stirring the building mix;

g.   Playing hockey with no club ☺

Usually work with the tool is to apply "jabs" to the soil with the sharp end of the instrument from up to down. After working with the "flat cutter" Fokin, the back does not hurt, and the soil is not damaged - by functionality it is quite suitable for the leading tool of permaculture man.

Pest control. Among agriculture pests, the biggest and the most widespread species remains, to my great regret, Homo Sapiens. Next on harmfulness are neighbor children, their dogs and, finally, birds and insects. If there are no problems with the Homo (not) Sapiens, as it were, (or rather, they should not have been), then some variants of quite effective relations are possible with birds, insects and other pests.

It is very important to understand what they want from your garden and how all the dirty work on their removal can be transferred to each other. It is good to know the faces of their enemies and try to attract them to your side. This, of course, is the most troublesome, but at the same time the most interesting part of the garden work.

Birds in the garden often play a dual role. The most useful are small inhabitants of forest and steppe zones who like to settle in hard-to-reach places - tall, thick and thorny crowns of trees and shrubs, in hollows, under roof ridge, etc. Others (starlings, for example), along with the benefits often cause damage to the crop, gluing fruit and berries. In this case, a grid with a shallow cell stretched over a ridge, will not only serve as additional watering (see above), but also protect it from their excessive appetite.

A very useful measure is the seasonal (mainly - autumn) poultry grazing on the fruit lands. The ubiquitous hens, for example, peck not only bugs and larvae, but also small seeds of weeds. The main thing is that they cannot reach the fruit or seeds and the first juicy vegetable sprouts, to which they, of course, are very eager.

There is also a great variety of dangerous and cunning enemies - from the simplest to the smallest creatures - and this is not necessarily insects. Recipes for fighting them are divided into biological and chemical, sometimes strictly individual, but there are also general principles. Obligatory conditions are the maintenance of biological diversity and the general ecological situation. The first implies the maximum number of elements of the landscape on your area - buildings, elements of improvement, plantations, ponds, lawns, stones, etc. It is especially important to have a variety of plantations - the largest possible number of species of trees, shrubs, flowering perennials and ground cover plants. If at least one piece of land remains unused, it will immediately begin to overgrow with weeds - because nature does not tolerate emptiness. The second condition includes a general agronomic background - the purity of soil, air, water in your locality and even a positive energy and mental situation (modern science knows very little about this yet).

Each poison has its own antidote, and in nature, man has more friends than enemies - otherwise he simply would not have survived. Good way to attract them is to build a special house. It looks like a birdhouse and at the same time an open bookshelf with two pitched roofs to protect it from precipitation.

If you can set the house in a place protected from wind and sun, you can leave it open on both sides. Otherwise, it is better to close the back side, so as not to bother insects with air currents. The house must also be secured and raised above the ground to protect it from moisture. The material for filling the "shelves" is a variety of waste - hollow dry stems of plants, bricks, wood cuttings (it is necessary to drill holes at the ends), straw, etc. A small "guide to the materials" is given below:

1. *Straw or wood*: this material will attract green lacewing, whose larvae feed on many pests: aphids, powdery mildew, whitefly, and mite eggs.

2. *Bamboo sticks*: provide shelter for solitary bees that pollinate the first flowers of fruit trees, starting in March.

3. *Inverted pots filled with hay*: it attracts the florists who love pests like aphids.

4. *Boards hidden behind metal plates*: attract insects involved in the decomposition of dead wood

5. *Trimming wood with holes*: they will become a popular shelter for many very useful pollinators, such as bees and single wasps, whose larvae feed on aphids.

6. *Tubular stems of blackthorn, elderberry, etc.*: provide housing for hoverflies and other hymenopterans.

7. *Brick with closed cells*: it attracts ladybirds that fly to spend the winter. Their larvae exterminate a lot of aphids.

Often, gardeners are annoyed by slugs and snails (especially in places with high humidity - in the lowlands, near water bodies, etc.). To combat them, you can cut a small hole on the three sides of the bottom of the plastic canister. The bent piece of plastic will serve as a bridge, and to attract creatures to the bottom, a little beer or wine is poured. Amphibians (frogs, frogs, snakes) and lizards also very much like to devour these creatures - therefore they should not be removed from the site in any way. The sweet smell of beer is not uncommonly attracted to the bears that sweat in it, as well as such exceptionally useful animals that the hedgehog is prickly. Hungarians, for example, specially put in their gardens small troughs, filled with weakly alcoholic beer to attract hedgehogs - they claim that it becomes even more angry with it and hunts for mice and slugs with redoubled energy.

As indispensable friends of the garden should also be mentioned bats and all who hunt for the larvae of pests under the earth - moles, shrews, etc. A huge role is played by insect pollinators cultivated by humans - bees and bumblebees. In fruit plantations, in the presence of all unfavorable factors, they contribute to an increase in the number of crops by at least a third.

Chemical weed and pest killers should be used as less as possible and only in case of emergency - with a sudden outbreak of pest abundance. Most often these drugs act like napalm - destroying all of the microflora and insects, harmful and useful. It is better to use protectors with a hazard class of not higher than IV and often change the form of the working protector. As a matter of fact, all the chemical means of our time is a stone age, and it is replaced by a completely different generation of means. For example, the development of a special neurolyptic peptide called "Natalezin", which regulates the sexual activity and insects reproductive ability. Natalizin consists of short chains of amino acids and is part of the fragrant alarm system of insects and arthropods. It acts selectively and affects only a specific type of pest. Blocking the active substance leads to the fact that the female sex prevents the courtship of males, and the males themselves do not seek to attract females. So far, these funds are in the final stages of experiments, but soon they should be expected to enter the market.

Permaculture people, as a rule, are united in groups and communities, where live communication and exchange of useful experience takes place. As the experience of the first ecological settlements has shown, children are eager to participate in garden work, sometimes carefully imitate adult's techniques and skills. For them, this is the first step in developing a living ecosystem and learning about the amazing world of plants and animals of which they are a part.

Of course, all that was stated above is only one of the facets of Knowledge. Many are lucky enough to learn and get to know much more amazing. And in order to open the reader only one detail of this fascinating puzzle piece, I will tell (no, better - I'll sing!) ode to only one species of plant life, namely:

Cannabis sativa:

The fact is that I do not know plants that are more useful, easy to grow and more unfairly forgotten by man than Cannabis sativa. In the process of the development of civilization this plant, sometimes covered with rumors and legends, had no less influence on the development of human civilization than, for example, wheat or corn. Ritual use of cannabis was spread already in the Neolithic in northern Asia and was used as a sacred attribute in the Ancient East. It was mentioned in the 19th and 20th volumes of Natural History by Pliny the Elder, Herodotus and the ancient Roman physician Pedanius Dioscorides in his work "De materia medica" ("On medicines").

According to the Polish researcher Sula Benet, cannabis called caneh bosm (which, in her opinion, was mistakenly translated as "ayr" or "sweet-smelling reed") is mentioned in the Old Testament as an ingredient of the holy anointing oil.

The geography of the plant does not end on this, and the history of its glorious adventure is just beginning. The flowering of the use of culture falls on the period between the fifteenth and twentieth centuries AD. In England, for example, it is considered so important that King Henry VIII in 1553 passed a law allowing fine farmers who could not grow at least a quarter of an acre of cannabis for every 60 acres of arable land they owned. History USA is obliged to it:

- o development of maritime trade (because 90% of sails and ropes of all vessels were made from cannabis);

- o 80% of the number of all textiles - fabrics, clothes, linens, curtains, bed linen until about 1820 (the beginning of the use of equipment for cleaning and processing cotton);

- o Refusing to grow cannabis in America in the 17th and 18th centuries was illegal! You could be imprisoned in the state of Virginia for refusing to cultivate the culture between 1763 and 1769 (source: "Cannabis in Colonial Virginia", GM Herdon). From 1631 to the early 1800s in the USA it was possible to pay taxes exclusively on cannabis. It is also known that in 1850 in the United States there were more than 8,300 hemp farms. Indians of the Lakota, blackfoot and Cherokee called it "the only good that the white man brought";

- o The first copies (drafts) of the US Constitution, the first Bibles, maps, schemes, the Betsy Ross flag(including the first drafts of the Declaration of Independence), and a lot of the first banknotes of money were printed on cannabis paper;

- o In 1916, the US government withdrew the forecast that by 1940 all the paper will be produced only from hemp and that no trees will be needed to be cut down for its production. Studies have shown that one acre of cannabis can produce as much raw fiber as it contains in 4.1 acres of plantations. Hemp cellulose is suitable for the production of very strong white paper, which serves an incredibly long time and does not turn yellow with time;

- o The first Model-T car Henry Ford was created to work on hemp gasoline, the engine consumed hemp oil and in general the whole machine was constructed from cannabis! On the territory of his large estate, Ford was photographed among his fields of this divine gift. The car "grown from the soil" was assembled from hemp plastic panels, which, according to the sources (the magazine "Popular Mechanics" 1941), were 10 times stronger than steel to counteract the impact force;

- o In the makeweight, it can be added that the first national flag of the USA and even the world's first jeans of "Levi * s" were sewn from hemp fibers.

It was the No. 1 plant in the export of many states and often an object of constant friction between them. For example, the war of 1812 between France and Russia was also carried out because the Emperor Napoleon wanted to cut off the export of hemp from Russia, the largest exporter of that time to continental England (source: "The Emperor does not wear any clothes" Jack Herer).

Do you know that by various estimates, cannabis has about 25,000 methods of application in our daily live? Starting from food, paint, clothing, fuel and building materials ...

... and ending with tea bags "Lipton" in which hemp fibers are also present. At one time it was called the "Corporation for a billion dollars" - it happened when its turnover in the world exceeded one billion (the magazine "Popular Mechanics", February 1938). Another magazine ("Mechanical Engineering" in February 1938) published an article entitled "The most profitable and desirable resource that can be grown." It developed the idea that, "if you cultivate cannabis using the technologies of the 20th century, it can become the largest agricultural crop in the US and around the world."

But this, unfortunately, did not happened. That ruthless stupidity and ignorance with which the glorious history of this culture ended can be rightfully called the World Conspiracy against cannabis. And it's not a new round of "industrial revolution", which replaced sailing navigation to steam, as some researchers believe. In addition, **the real reason for declaring a culture outlawed has nothing common with its impact on the mind and body!** Hemp as a whole is not harmful to the human body or mind. And even so-called "Marijuana" does not pose a threat to the general public - therefore, it is actually legalized in the Netherlands. But its application, and especially Cannabis seed, is very dangerous for energy companies, alcoholic, tobacco industry and a large number of chemical corporations. The truth is, first of all, if hemp were used in a wide range of commercial products, it would eventually lead to an industrial revolution! But at the same time it destroyed many modern businesses, first of all, the sacred cow of the system - Oil.

This only resource could save thousands of human souls from starving death, save tens of thousands of hectares of tropical forest and create millions of new workplaces, generate billions of products of quality. However, in 1937 the heirs of Dupont patented a number of production processes that marked the arrival of the whole era of fossil energy sources on the scene. (* According to the Toxic 100 rankings, formed by the Political Economy Research Institute (USA), in August 2013, DuPont was on the 1 st place among the companies that pollute the environment in the United States). On the annual report, the chairman urged the shareholders to invest in the new division of "petrochemistry" all available funds. Synthetic materials such as plastics, cellophane, celluloid, methanol, nylon, viscose, lavsan, etc. are now produced, mainly from oil, gas and other hydrocarbons. Industrialization in agriculture, innovations in the production of cannabis would destroy more than 80% of DuPont's business.

During these years, someone Andrew Mellon became a

secretary of the State Treasury and the main investor of DuPont. He appointed his nephew Harry J. Anslinger to head the Federal Bureau of Narcotics and Dangerous Drugs.

It is known that these financial magnates held a series of secret meetings. Cannabis seed was declared dangerous and posing a threat to their enterprises. In order for their dynasties to remain intact, it had to disappear from industry. These people took an obscure Mexican slang word: "marijuana" and pushed it into the minds of America ... The subsequent defamation and juggling of facts about the ancient culture in the media of that time is a topic for a separate conversation.

In order to present to the wide circle of readers all the groundlessness of these charges, it is necessary to plunge deeper into the physiology of this plant.

Cannabis sativa is a genus of annual plants of the Cannabaceae family. At present, according to the classification of American scientists E. Small and A. Cronquist, this plant is divided into two types: Cannabis sativa subsp. Sativa and Cannabis sativa subsp. Indica (Lam.) - each with its own varieties. They differ in appearance (sowing is much higher) the conditions of growth and some morphological features. This bad reputation that is attributed to "marijuana" belongs precisely to Indian Hindus and not to the sowing, which, in fact, we are considering.

So, our culture has two types of flowers and often distinguish two types of individuals - male and female, slightly different in structure and functions (there are also bisexual varieties). In female plants, flowers are collected in a complex ear and give in consequence fruits - small seeds-nuts with very valuable properties. In males, the flowers are collected in friable and odorous panicles, and the stems have a stronger fibrous structure. Psychoactive components are contained only in resinous color allocation - in Cannabis Indica in larger quantities, in Sowing - in much less.

The content of this narcotic substance (the so-called "delta nine THC") in Cannabis sowing according to the current world standards should not exceed 0.2% in raw materials (in different countries this figure may differ). Currently, a large number of varieties of this plant are created in the world, containing "delta nine" in a much lower concentration. (And if genetics seriously tackled this problem, they could generally reduce this number to zero - author's note). Such requirements are met, for example, by the varieties of Polish breeding created at the Institute of Natural Fibers in Poznan which are called: Białobrzeskie, Beniko, Silesia, Tygra, Rajan, Wojko. They belong to the forms characteristic of middle Europe, hence their period of vegetation is adapted to the Polish soil and climatic conditions. These species have a height of over 2 meters, typically the fibrous structure of the stem, have a psychotropic content of less than 0.2%.

Therefore, not everything is lost. It is only necessary to create a transnational corporation that will only deal with the seed under the new flag of the Green Revolution. It will require extensive investment and branding of new products, which more often are only well-forgotten old ones.

However, let us return to the subject of the conversation and try to cover all the main issues on the topic of cultivation and the production of goods from crops.

Cannabis sativa is not exacting to the conditions of growth within its range of growth and in fact, does not suffer from anything. It is considered a river valleys and lowlands plant, therefore it prefers soils rich in humus, nitrogen and calcium, weakly alkaline or neutral. On light sandy and heavy clay soils yields much smaller plants; also avoid places with excessive moisture. Especially likes to grow on virgin land - in this case it drowns out even the most enduring weeds.

Farmers love this culture for its unpretentiousness, rapid growth and high yields. People who are engaged in it, half-jokingly talk about it, that this is one of the few plants "which can be planted once, and then forgotten (before collection)." Hemp starts very powerful deep roots, so it does not suffer, as a rule, from moisture deficiencies. Remains of roots and green mass (leaves) after processing are well decomposed and improve the mechanical composition of the soil. It does not require treatment with herbicides to protect the shoots from weeds and can withstand frosts up to   -5 * C. Repels some malicious pests of potatoes and cabbage, so it is useful to plant between the rows of these vegetables. Can be grown in one place up to 4-5 years, but then still, requires a crop rotation due to the accumulation of fungi and small pests.

In recent years, scientists have discovered another remarkable property of this fantastic plant - the ability to draw from the soil toxic substances. Studies have shown that cannabis can be extremely useful in removing cadmium and other toxic metals from soil, as well as absorbing radiation. Experiments on the use of this unique property are being conducted the at Fukushima accident (Japan), and in Ukraine and Belarus - in the Chernobyl region. Belarusian scientists developments revealed that harvested after cultivation on the contaminated territory of the C. planting can be fully used for the production of biofuel.

Now a few words about the cultivation of our crops. After choosing a place for growing, you should decide - why do we need to grow this plant? Depending on the final product (seeds, cellulose, fibers), the variety, rates and timing of sowing, etc. are selected. For example, for sowing plantations it is recommended to sow 10-15 kg / ha and a row spacing of 50 cm. For other tasks, sowing is much thicker - 7.5 -15 cm between rows, and the number of seeds depends on the purpose of processing and ranges from 40 to 70 kg / ha : 30-40 kg / ha - to produce cellulose and 60-70 kg / ha - textile fibers.

All the subtleties of culture cultivation are covered in special literature and require, of course, a separate article. I will not dwell on this in detail, I will only note that in cultivated soils weakened after cultivation requires complex fertilizers (nitrogen-phosphorus-potassium), on acidified soils, 15-20 kg / ha of CaO * (* For soil-climatic conditions in Poland - author's comment).

On average, about 120 warm days are required for culture maturation * (* in Poland - author's note), and in August-September harvesting takes place. To obtain seeds, harvesting is performed a little later than for obtaining fibers. Of males, the fiber is of a higher quality; They are collected, when the plant after the flowering will turn yellow and discard the leaves, but the stem itself will not have time to completely dry out.

Hemp is squinted at 10 cm height - this can be done manually on small plots or by mechanical equipment on large ones - with the help of mowing machines, reapers, knitters, seed separators, etc.

Application of cannabis (main sections):

1. *Textile industry:* used for the production of fibers of very high quality. Of lighter and thinner raw materials are produced threads and fabrics. They are not as thin as, for example, linen or cotton, but they have remarkable properties - they are natural, breathable, hardy and resistant to thermal effects. Like natural textiles, it guarantees a constant body temperature both in cooler and warmer days. But in old days they were appreciated mainly for their great resistance to constant dampness, contact with sea or plain water - where other clothes soon disappeared at the seams, hemp remained for a long time unharmed. This remarkable feature is widely used in the manufacture of fire hoses, surgical threads and filter paper, as well as sports mats and non-woven fabric. For medical purposes it is highly recommended for people suffering from

allergies and skin rashes. This is where the application of the material does not end at all - because the coarser fiber that is obtained during processing goes to making ropes, sacks and wonderful tourist tents for cruises along the sea coast.

2. *Manufacture of paper and paperboard:* so-called "hemp straw" contains about 25-30% fiber (of the total plant mass) containing 70% of cellulose. This makes it an excellent raw material for the production of paper. At the same time, the annual growth of cellulose produced by the plant is 2.5 times higher than the increase in the same amount of cellulose obtained from wood. If we take the volume of one tree, which grew 100 years and compare it with the volume of plant mass of cannabis, which has grown over the same period, we get a quantity that is 305 times higher than the original! As a result, hemp paper is more durable and of a higher quality than the usual one - woody. And this is no longer a small penny, but a full-fledged pound into the piggy bank of the nature preservtion! Hemp fiber can also be used in the process of waste paper recycling or as an element enhancing the quality of paper.

3. *Constructing:* hemp waste after processing is used as a filler for walls, as well as for the production of extruded building boards and so-called "hemp concrete" (hempcrete technology). Hemp fiber is sometimes used as a filler for various cables, material for the production of wallpaper and as an

insulating material. Another, more important field of application remains the production of natural paints, varnishes and thinners. Hemp oil dries quickly and leaves a thin, elastic layer on the surface of objects - that's why it is so loved by artists and artisans.

4. *Food:* Think about it – every 3.6 seconds someone in the world dies of hunger. Nuts (cannabis seeds) may well become the most nutritious and economical solution to this problem. Their minimum starter package includes:

> – all 20 amino acids, including nine irreplaceable, that is, those that the human body does not produce;
>
> – a large number of simple proteins that increase immunity and resistance to toxins;
>
> – the highest concentration of basic fatty acids in the plant world, exceeding the similar index of any nuts or seeds, including flax seeds;
>
> – an ideal ratio of omega-6 and omega-3 acids, invaluable for the health of the cardiovascular and immune system of the human body;

The seeds of cannabis are among the best sources of digestible vegetable protein. They also have many nutrients that support the normal state of tissues, blood vessels, skin cells and other organs. And, finally, it is the richest source of basic fatty acids. Add to this the richness of mineral salts (especially zinc compounds), vitamins (A, D, K), lecithin, mucus, associated proteins and other important nutrition components – and you get even a far from complete picture of their nutritional value. In Poland hemp oil is used as an indispensable addition to lush Christmas dishes, and nuts have always been used in the traditional soup "siemieniotka". Flour from Cannabis sativa due to high protein content can be a wonderful supplement to other flour, for example barley or wheat.

5. *Treatment and body care:* in medicine, hemp is used in the cases of cancer, Alzheimer's disease, sclerosis, pain, burns and digestive problems. Seeds of Cannabis sativa contain the salt "fitin", so they help in the treatment of hysteria, neurasthenia, rickets and anemia. It is also recommended for those who are weakened, exhausted by the disease, suffering from avitaminosis. It is suitable as an analgesic, hypnotic and diuretic. Also, cannabis helps with insomnia, nausea and depression. Seed oil, used also in cosmetics, for example, for the production of creams, emulsions, oils and soaps, etc.

6. *Petrochemistry and the automotive industry:* hemp is used to make important parts of modern vehicles - instrument panels, tires and some other items of equipment. A mixture of oil from hemp and methanol serves as a substitute for oil in diesel engines. In the combustion process, it produces 70% less soot than oil from naphtha and does not contain substances that damage the biosphere.

7. *Animal and bird maintenance:* Waste that appears in the seed separation process is an excellent feed for animals on farms. Remnants of hemp straw after separation of fibers serve as the best bedding for livestock, as well as an effective floor covering for work in greenhouses. Crushed cannabis seeds are a very valuable component of bird food.

8. *Ecology:* hemp sowing along with the plant Paulownia felt, or the Imperial tree (Latin: Paulównia tomentósa) is ready to serve humanity in the reclamation of polluted and depleted non-rational use of land. The abandonment of processing waste on the soil enriches it with natural organic matter; Deep roots loosen and improve its mechanical composition. The earth is liberated from poisonous cadmium and lead compounds (indispensable attributes of automobile exhausts), and 1 hectare of cannabis crops binds about 2.5 tons of carbon dioxide - the main cause of the "greenhouse effect" of the planet.

At present, a huge number of entrepreneurs from all over the world are already seriously looking into this culture with a glorious past and a lot of promising future. Sometimes very ridiculous, sometimes excessively stringent barriers to the lawmaking of individual countries serve as an obstacle. Cannabis crops are prescribed to be protected by such forces that the process of growing it becomes not cost-effective. But even this does not stop individual enthusiasts and they build their own business on this. In Poland, for example, having overcome all bureaucratic obstacles, a program was organized called "The road of hemp and flax" in the ecological farm "Na Karczaku" (www.karczak.pl). This is a growing area of "ecological tourism" in Eastern Europe. It offers everyone an acquaintance not only with the process of cultivation of ancient cultures, but also the opportunity to participate in the work of certain trades related to them. On the territory of the economy there is a weaving workshop, where tourists and simply curious people practice in the manufacture of household goods – taking away the "made-for-yourself" item made by own hands. Also, the owners of the farm grow seeds for breeding, feeding birds, share their experience and give advice.

As one friend of mine said: "Cannabis is a trump card in my sleeve." Whoever and how did not relate to this culture, this does not detract from its significance and value for mankind. I believe that after all the above, I no longer need to campaign for it? ☺

Chapter 6: Greenhouses, the idea of which is simple like smoke: we transfer part of the maintenance costs to the account of nature.

This will be a very small chapter on the thematic continuation of our house. A place where you can safely meditate or just relax, lying quietly in a hammock after a hard working day. And not without benefit for the household. With the help of this equipment, you can heat your house additionally, grow food and even try to establish a very profitable business.

I do not know what my readers think about it, but I always dreamed of a winter garden – a kind of small green oasis in the middle of ice silence. I think, a lot of people need a mink such as a garage, attic or club, where you can dive into and no one will find you. As a solution, I propose a thermos - a greenhouse of buried type with the possibility of creating a small closed and self-sufficient ecosystem of life support.

Recently, a large number of start-uppers turned to the topic of getting organic and inexpensive food without leaving home. Small hit parade of these ideas from different corners of the planet is presented to your attention:

- o Recently, researchers from SolutionEra (Canada) have released a step-by-step guide on how to build a passive solar greenhouse that uses renewable energy from natural and recycled materials. "We believe that if we integrate the construction of our greenhouse with other technologies, such as compost heating, hydroponics and other intensive cultivation technologies, we will be able to grow most of the food on a sustainable basis, even in the coldest countries," say the developers. The very concept of passive solar greenhouses has become a logical continuation of 40 years' research in the field of the EarthShip underground buildings by Michael Reynolds, as well as many other studies on solar heaters. It includes the use of passive solar panels, thermal mass, geothermal energy, rainwater and heat pumps.

- o Architect Bengt Varn from Sweden designed and built for the Marie Granmar and Charles Sacilotto family (who wanted to build an energy-saving house from scratch), double slope dome greenhouse made of metal and glass. They covered their country house as a magician covers a rabbit with a hat, and now they have fresh vegetables all year round – besides, in the conditions of severe Scandinavian winter. Naturhus (Natural Home) - this is how the architect calls his designs, and he built the first such house back in 1974.

  Such solar thermos is not just a romantic extension to the house. The family now saves on heating and is completely independent of the city sewage system. Plus, they have an eternal summer and sunbathing lying on the roof of her house in a comfortable environment.

- o It is beneficial to use greenhouses not only in countries with cold climate, but also in conditions of hot Africa. This was recently proved by a group of researchers from North Ethiopia with a very simple technological design. The project called "Roots Up" was developed by a nonprofit organization that is a part of the Gondar University. The pyramidal greenhouse, which collects air moisture, is designed to help farmers grow fresh vegetables even during drought periods. Special traps release hot air and moisture during the heat of the day creating a better atmosphere for plant growth, and then the upper part of the greenhouse opens at night, which captures cool air, collecting condensate at the dew point. Drops of water are sent to the tank and can be used as drinking water or for irrigation. This design can also be used as a reservoir for collecting rainwater during the rain. For assembly, only inexpensive materials are used, so the operation of such device justifies its price:

(https://www.youtube.com/watch?v=UPiCoKL2hzU).

o In countries with a cold climate, the costs of heating large greenhouses are sometimes 60-70% of the production cost. For the agrarians Poland, this is often an inadequate burden. For growing vegetables, they use two pitched tunnel type greenhouses, in which a lot of technical solutions are used to save heat: fans, curtains, two-layer film coating, temperature control systems in combination with water storage tanks, etc. But significantly some of the heat still flows outward with the air. Scientists from Krakow and Skernevichy have been working for many years to find the solution of the problem. In 2010 - 2015, they created a natural battery, which is laid under the base of the greenhouse and forcedly circulates the air. To preserve heat, the best suitable material is used - natural stone (porphyry granules), with particle sizes of about 30-63 mm. Technological innovation in the design is the use of three independent parts of the battery, which make it possible to store and reuse even a small amount of warm air. Thanks to it, scientists managed to extend the vegetation period for a whole month.

- The creative approach to the case was shown by the architectural studio Salt & Water from Belgrade (Slovenia). They developed a functional floating barge-greenhouse on the Danube river, which is capable of providing energy and growing organic-pure food products. In addition to energy and vegetables, this floating construction can also serve as a platform for the formation and development of ecological communities. The floating structure consists of a greenhouse with vertical cages at one end and a small building on the other. Solar panels and non-large wind turbines generate electricity and run an effective irrigation system that provides moisture to the plant. According to the calculations of the architects, the greenhouse can work year-round, constantly moving in search of the best lighting and temperature. A good solution for the constantly growing prices for land in large cities, isn't it?

- For a medium-sized household, there is one very simple solution that has been used for centuries in the cold mountain regions of South America (Peru,

Ecuador, etc.). Indians who call this "walipini" ("a place for heat") use it not only for growing vegetables, but also for keeping goats in the cold season. In Central Asia, similar devices are used to grow citrus seedlings. Greenhouses (winter gardens) in noblemen's estates of Russia were also built with the necessary deepening of the foundation - in order that the roots of plants growing on the "bottom" would be much lower than the horizon of freezing of the soil in winter. Such greenhouses used the principle of "omshanica" (omshanic - a structure for the bees wintering) and required much lower costs for heating and lighting than standard greenhouses on the surface. Such winter garden has survived to the present day in the estate of one famous vegetarian, writer Leo Tolstoy in Yasnaya Polyana.

In order that the winter garden would bring the maximum effect, it is necessary to meet a number of conditions. They are not complicated at all, but they require a competent approach:

1. For the location of the greenhouse choose the sunniest place - the southern or south-western side of the house. In this case, not neighboring buildings nor large trees should shade the upper, light-passing panel. The length of the pit under the greenhouse should be oriented to the sides of the world from east to west. It is also necessary to perform geological prospecting for the level of groundwater and flood waters in the

spring. The probability of flooding the hothouse is much higher in areas with a lower relief.

2. It is good, if the back (more elevated) wall of the greenhouse will be simultaneously the front wall of the house - then you can save on construction materials additionally, and also promote mutual heating of premises. If this cannot be achieved constructively, it is better to insulate the northern side of the roof in order to save precious calories in the winter. In this case, the angle of inclination of roof panels should have an optimum value of about 40 degrees - then the sunlight will fall at right angles, and the fallen snow will not stay long on the surface.

3. Peruvian greenhouses are the simplest type of winter gardens. Its walls are slightly inclined to

prevent soil shedding, but this does not help with prolonged downpours. A more complex and at the same time more efficient option is the construction of a tunnel-type thermos of a tunnel type with a natural drainage system and a significant reduction in heat losses.

Greenhouses of this type are arranged like an ordinary tourist thermos (with a glass bulb inside the plastic case), i.e. have two rows of walls between which a granular insulation, gravel or expanded clay is poured-in short, everything that is capable of effectively passing water through itself. The outer wall is the soil slightly inclined to the base (as in the Peruvian greenhouse), but an internal vertical partition made of any building material - brick, sheet slate or gypsum boards.

4. All the moisture that flows down the roof of the greenhouse falls into the interlayer between the walls of the structure and thus falls into the base - a pillow made of the same material (insulation) on which the fertile layer is filled and vegetables grow. More clever solution is to create an additional layer of biological material capable of decomposition - for example, fallen leaves, mown grass, fresh manure, etc. As it is known from agrochemistry lessons, the process of organic matter decay is accompanied by the release of heat and enriches the soil with nutrients. Thus, we considerably save on heating in the winter season. So, we apply "raised

ridges" or ridges of Jacob R. Mittleider (see chapter 5) in their greenhouse where the plants are located on a drain cushion (about 20 cm thick) of expanded clay or rubble with a fraction of not more than 3 cm in diameter, layer from organic materials spilled with an aqueous solution of effective microorganisms (10-15 cm) and a layer of nutrient compost (not less than 5 cm). Drainage almost always contains moisture, therefore, plants will always reach for it, growing a powerful root system and an aerial part with Additional fruits. To remove excess moisture, which sometimes occur during strong and prolonged downpours, the lowest point of the greenhouse should form a water receiver with a drainage submersible pump and a hose that leads out water. Receiver for convenience is arranged in the form of a box of simple, but strong metal mesh with small cells. It is better to purchase a pump with a float for automatic switching on and off - then you will not need to constantly monitor this process.

5. Internal walls of the greenhouse are recommended to be treated with a material for hydro-isolation from the side of the filled drainage - this will protect it from destruction and snow mold. Under the drainage cushion, insulation is also desirable, unless the soil under it consists only from clay that has the property of "locking" water.

6. In the greenhouse it is absolutely necessary to maintain the temperature regime and to circulate the air - forced or natural. It should be remembered that cold air is always heavier than warm air, so it will concentrate in the lower layers near the surface of the earth. If the sunlight reaches the surface, it heats the soil, which, in turn, heats the air nearby. It becomes lighter and rushes upward, displacing the colder air. So the natural air circulation is carried out. Various equipment is used for forced circulation, which is less preferred because of high cost. For a small greenhouse, it is enough:

* In the warm season - two or three removable panels (window pane) in the upper part of the structure. If the temperature exceeds the value of 20-25 * C, as much of the moisture-containing items as possible are bringing into the room - pallets with wet sand, troughs, etc. Evaporation, moisture reduces the temperature in the lower layer of air.

* In the cold season, it is sometimes necessary to maintain the temperature artificially, using various devices for heating. In this case, the most rational and environmentally friendly solution to the problem seems to me the electrical thermo panels with a sensor - the air temperature regulator, located in the lowest part of the greenhouse walls. It is responsible for the optimum temperature level, switching the panels

on when cooling and shutting them down after heating the air. It should be remembered that for the overwhelming number of vegetables, fruits and houseplants, the temperature at 10-15 * C in the winter season is adequate for normal vegetation and fruiting. For plants of the subtropical and tropical zone, this bar increases to 20-25 * C and requires a higher moisture level. Thicker glass, double glazed windows and an increase in the thickness of channel polycarbonate in the upper part of the structure also contribute to a significant preservation of heat in the winter.

Both plants and people who will stay and work in the greenhouse certainly have a need in fresh air intake to prevent stagnant phenomena. For this purpose, it is equipped with 1-2 pieces of PVC pipes 20 cm in diameter with holes cut out at the bottom. They are placed vertically in the corners of the guys, and their upper part is taken out. If necessary, all seams of pipe joints are sealed with mounting foam.

7. In winter, when the length of the day is shorter, the plants in the greenhouse need additional illumination. For this, it is rational to use an economical LED daylight spectrum lamp with an ambient light sensor that turns the light on and off. The reflective foil glued to the raised part of the inner wall helps not only to keep heat, but also increases the amount of illumination inside

the greenhouse. If the northern roof slope is not transparent, then it is insulated with expanded polystyrene plates, and then also glued with foil. Calculation of the number of lamps and connections is determined depending on the lighting standards that are applied to plants in greenhouses (provided a year round cycle of cultivation). As practice shows, a greenhouse thermos with dimensions of 5 to 20 m. consumes up to 10 kW/h in the cold season.

8. Connection of the greenhouse to the water supply is carried out in two ways - expensive and rational. The first method is simpler, but also the most expensive in terms of resources: drilling a well near a greenhouse, or using existing communications on the area. The second implies the use of the methods described in chapter 5, which are used for irrigation, with an amendment to the underground subsistence. To do this, it is necessary to collect and store rainwater and thawed water in plastic reservoirs if possible, and to provide for the removal of surplus moisture from the pits by means of a pump (see point 3) in these tanks.

The tanks are equipped with a pre-filter and are connected to the drip irrigation system of the plants. It is also possible to add an aqueous solution of mineral fertilizers with microelements to the tank. So that's how the whole scheme of irrigation looks briefly.

The nutrient substrate in the greenhouse also needs to be

updated and "revitalized" every year, after growing the crop. The compost must be approximately equal to the weight of the produced product.

 Now you can safely do more pleasant and essential things - for example, growing dwarf trees or creating a collection of rare plants. Ukrainian breeder Patiy Anatoly Vasilyevich from the Rozhny village, which is near Kiev, made this a lifelong work and built a whole business on it. In the greenhouse-thermos developed and patented by him, more than 50 varieties of tropical plants grow, not at all typical in this climatic zone (some of them are derived by the farmer). Pineapples, papaya, bananas, coffee and even tomato trees - this is not a complete list of plants that grow in his greenhouse.

The seedlings of the banana "Super Dwarf" bred by a

scientist are only 80 cm long (in nature they grow up to 3.5 meters). He is the only who own this strain and there is no else in the world - at the same time they can be placed in the bedroom and they will bear fruit. The price of this "miracle" is only from 50 to 500 hryvna (about 6.25 - 62.5 $ USA). Anatoliy Vasilievich also widely uses vaccinations, "Chinese" or air way of rooting and strongly recommends using grafted lemons in his home environment. According to him, they are agitating the air with phytoncides, and children in the family are starting to get sick less.

"What I do, allows me to travel around the world" - says the scientist. "This business does not require hard work, but people do not want to know this. More than a hundred thousand people came here - and many left empty-handed. We actively take care of the plants three months a year, the rest of the time - we travel, we spend time in our pleasure. "

Quite good information for reflection, is it not?

Chapter 7: Self-sufficient human environment is possible on Earth!

Imagine that you have become a hostage to a difficult situation. Output like in a spaceship - only in outer space, or the crew must device under the existing provisions and try to become an indispensable and useful in the workplace. Does it not remind you of anything?

Life on the planet Earth is like a one-way ticket, a fascinating journey or run with obstacles. It is necessary to determine the status, its role and purpose on this submarine or spaceship floating under the Sun. Who are we – one- hour visitors? Hostages of events? Owners, guests or dependents? Damage from the beginning, or all-mighty without end? All further events depend only on the coordinated actions of the whole crew. We are able to threaten the boat in which we sail? Or we are able to treat the planet as our own home - improving the interior, making repairs, not breaking, not clogging or destroying anything around...

Yes, so far there are more questions than answers, and there is a suspicion that this will always be so. We are not the first who are interested in it. Richard Buckminster Fuller, a great dreamer and professional architect, throughout his life wondered if humanity has a chance of a long-term and successful survival on the planet Earth and, if so, how. Considering himself an ordinary person without any savings or academic degree, he decided to devote his life to this issue, he tried to find out what individuals like him can do to improve the condition of mankind. Fuller understood that large corporations, governments or private enterprises can not do this because of their predators and parasites nature. In 1927, at the age of 32, practically without money and work, he lived in a cheap apartment in Chicago (Illinois). At this time, Richard Buckminster's beloved daughter Alexandra died as a result of pneumonia. Feeling responsible for what happened, he abuses alcohol, which quickly leads him to the brink of suicide. Yes, this person had very good reasons to find the easiest way, as it seemed to him at that moment, to get out of the circle of problems. But like no one else, he understood that in this life the participation is not that important, but victory. Therefore, at the last moment he decides to arrange an experiment instead of death to "*see what one man can do for the benefit of the world and all mankind*".

In the next half century, Buckminster Fuller presented the world with a wide range of ideas, developments and inventions, especially in the areas of practical low-cost housing and transportation. Since 1947, he has been developing the spatial construction of the "geodesic dome", which is a hemisphere assembled from tetrahedron that will bring him international recognition and fame (in 1959, under the name "golden dome", it will be built for the American National Exhibition in Moscow, and in 1967 - in the US pavilion at the World Exhibition in Montreal). The scientist predicted that human societies would soon rely mainly on renewable energy sources, such as electricity from sunlight and wind energy. He hoped for the advent of the era of *"successful education and the security of mankind"*.

Richard Buckminster Fuller received 25 US patents and many honorary scientific degrees, was a laureate of 47 international and American awards in the field of architecture, design, engineering, fine arts and literature. In 1970, he receives Gold Medal from the American Institute of Architects, and travels the whole world, giving lectures to students and teaching at universities. This great man lived to an honorable old age and at the age of 87 died almost in one day with his wife, leaving behind a great legacy in the form of books, scientific works, essays and a whole galaxy of followers and admirers.

So, friends, if it suddenly seems that the sky is only gray, and the world around is a shit, remember this story and take off your hat in honor of this Great Dreamer, who did not submit to destiny. Let his example be just a drop in the ocean. "But from drops the oceans are composed" - as it was said in one of the films.

Yes, it is a lot of bad, it is offensive and always on display. Great villains are sometimes as famous as great geniuses, and politicians and businessmen make money both on good advertising and reputation, and on bad. But does this somehow reduce Good, make it less quality? Therefore, Good (in the parables of King Solomon this is called "wisdom") is no less in this world - otherwise this planet Earth has not yet stood on its axis, and man has not enjoyed what he saw. It's just hidden from the eyes, we look for it as for pearl and rejoice, like finding gold. We all live for it, this is the cornerstone of our Future, which is simply doomed to Abundance and Prosperity in the best way. These are the two main subjects that Mother Nature teaches us.

Of course, you noticed that over and under the sky reign ergonomics, proportionality and order - the basis of design. Their diversity and degree of development give rise to the greatness of Chaos, an impressive soul and connecting patterns. We can only find our place in this boat, and lean on the oars.

About the place and role of a person in Space is taught not only by parents from Japan, whose families, according to travelers, have the most obedient children all over the world. The community of people gave birth to a new paradigm of the terrestrial biosphere, which was called "noosphere" in the writings of Professor Vernadsky from Russia. At present, this reality is very poorly harmonized with the surrounding space, sometimes entering into a distinct dissonance with the environment. The state of things on the planet significantly undermines the overall balance of vital resources. According to the level of energy industry development, humanity is in the zero development cycle ("палка-костер" примитивного человека or "burning energy") and is just preparing to move to the first class of renewable energy sources. According to the level of development of morality, modern man also is not far from the time of the Neolithic cave, where an individual of different tribe and different understanding of basic values often became an additional meat for an evening dinner. To the end, the problem of productive recycling and income distribution has not been solved. The most important factor for development is the lack of free time and the global problem of loneliness.

More than one generation of scholars and thinkers are arguing about the role and place of the rational man in the Earth's biosphere. But the history of mankind cannot be copied from a white sheet. We will all be glad to get into the primordial Paradise, but our sins are not allowed us to go there. To test this experimentally in the early 90s, a group of volunteer scientists decided to create a closed and autonomous biosystem under sealed domes and live there for 2 years.

The experiment was named "Biosphere-2", and the main sponsor and initiator of the idea was American billionaire Ed Bass from Texas. The development of structures and systems took about 10 years, during this time, special groups of scientists collected across the Earth a variety of species of animals and plants to populate the station, search for soil samples, carefully ensuring that everything there was preserved the necessary biological balance.

Glass modules included almost everything necessary for life: the jungle, savanna, swamp and even a small ocean with a beach and a coral reef. More than 3000 plant species from all over the world were planted. Also inside were launched about 4 thousand diverse representatives of fauna, including goats, pigs and chickens on the farm. The settlement was like a planet Earth in miniature, untouched by a technical civilization, where 8 enlightened people planned to engage in simple physical work, gather at a dinner table, work for a great goal and for the benefit of science. One of the goals of the mission was to confirm the self-sufficiency of man-made habitat without any outside help. Even the air exchange was maintained by a special valve system, and only electricity came from outside. However, the settlers did not take into account a number of circumstances and did not consider necessary to cooperate with scientists, ecologists, chemists, and physicists, but approached the experiment process as a fun or entertaining show.

At first everything was just as they had dreamed. The colonists worked enthusiastically on the farm fields, checked the operation of all systems, followed the turbulent life of the jungle, fished, sat on their own small beach, and at evening they ate a superbly cooked dinner on the balcony. His colonists nicknamed the "Visionary Cafe" - hence the future seemed especially bright. After dinner, philosophical discussions or improvised jam sessions on musical instruments were arranged. But about a week later the chief technician of the Biosphere, Van Tillo, came to breakfast very excited. He announced that he had strange and unpleasant news. Daily measurements of the air condition showed that the designers of the dome were mistaken in the calculations. In the atmosphere, the amount of oxygen was gradually reduced and the percentage of carbon dioxide increased. While it was completely invisible, but if the trend continues, in about a year the existence at the station will become impossible. From that day, the paradisiacal life of the settlers was over, and a tense struggle began for the air they breathed.

But people decided not to give up. It was decided to devote all free time to planting and caring for plants. Secondly, they have launched at full capacity the reserve absorber of carbon dioxide, from which it was necessary to clean up the sediment. An unexpected assistant was the ocean, which absorbed some of the CO_2. It should be noted that this happens in nature, although many do not notice this. It is the World Ocean that represents the lungs of our planet (rather, single-celled and simple organisms living in the upper layers of the water), and not just the Amazonian selva and the jungle, as some think. But some of the compounds are converted to acetic acid, gradually increasing the acidity of the ocean. With the similar collided and colonists, who had to use additives that lower it. However, this did not help, and the air under the dome became more sparse. Soon another global problem arose before them. It turned out that the farm is about 2000 m². With all modern technologies of processing the earth is able to provide only 80% of the needs of colonists in food. Their daily diet (the same for women and men) was 1,700 calories, which is normal for a sedentary office life, but is catastrophically small with the amount of physical work that every resident of "Biosphere-2" was supposed to perform.

One evening, expert Jane Pointer responsible for the farm admitted that she was aware of the future food crisis. A few months before the settlement, she calculated that the colonists would not have enough food, but under the influence of Dr. Walford it was decided that this shortage would only benefit them. And indeed, after six months of the "hungry" diet, the blood of the settlers has improved significantly - the cholesterol level has decreased, the metabolism has improved. People lost 10 to 18 percent of their body weight and looked surprisingly young. But at the same time they felt worse and worse, although they continued to smile through the glasses to curious journalists.

The 1992 season was especially difficult for the colonists. These were the consequences of a hurricane on El Niño, because of which the sky over "Biosphere-2" was clouded almost all winter long. Weak light weakened the photosynthesis of the jungle (hence, the production of precious oxygen), and reduced the already poor yields. All rice crops were destroyed by pests, and their diet for several months almost entirely consisted of beans, sweet potatoes and carrots. With an excess of beta-carotene in the body, their skin gradually acquired an orange color.

Soon came the denouement. Everything collapsed and broke, and the world around them lost its beauty and harmony. In the "desert" because of the condensation on the ceiling it regularly rained, so that many cacti rotted. The huge five-meter high mountains in the jungle suddenly became brittle, like rotten matches. They fell, crashing everything around. (Subsequently, investigating this phenomenon, scientists came to the conclusion that its cause was covered in the absence of wind under the dome, which strengthens tree trunks in nature.) The sewage in fish ponds was clogged with silt, and the fish became less and less. The animal world of the jungle and savanna also inexorably contracted. Only cockroaches and ants, which filled all possible places, felt perfectly. The man-made biosphere of people was gradually dying.

On September 26, 1993, the experiment had to be stopped when the oxygen level inside the complex reached 15%, at a rate of 21%. People went out into the fresh air. They were weakened and embittered. In 2011, the buildings were purchased by the University of Arizona to continue research. Now there are visiting studios, and more than 10,000 schoolchildren visit the Biosphere every year.

Completely exploring the causes of the phenomena occurring at the station, the scientists came to all sorts of curious discoveries. It turned out that the cement overlaps of the domes played a fatal role, which reacted with oxygen and formed oxides. Another reason for the lack of oxygen was the breathing of simple organisms in soil and the atmosphere, which multiplied greatly during the experiment. For some reason, everyone forgot about them.

However, it does not matter. The experiment only demonstrated the genius and indispensability of the creation of the Lord, which man cannot repeat for the present. On one of the inner walls of this lost Paradise, there are still several lines written by one of the women: "Only here we felt how dependent on the surrounding nature. If there are no trees - we will not have anything to breathe, if the water gets dirty - we will not have anything to drink." So it was not in vain - they made the right conclusions. Further research in this area continues to this day. Everyone understands perfectly well that the future of mankind is beyond the cosmos, and this presupposes a constant finding of a man in an autonomous environment he artificially created. In this regard, more successful were the development of Russian scientists I .A. Terskov and I. I. Gitelzon. In the course of their research ("BIOS-1, 2, 3"), it became possible to create closed systems of human life support. Their work ceased in the years of Perestroika and again continued only in 2005 with the support of the European Space Agency (ESA) in Krasnoyarsk, Russia.

Since 1991, the International Center for Closed Ecological Systems has been operating there, which, simultaneously with the Lunar Palace in China, is studying the problems of creating an artificial biosphere.

Let's try to understand why this is so important for each of us. In reality, this represents the world, in which we all live. What is called the environment, evolved over three and a half billion years of evolution and turned into a stable connected system - a cycle of substances. Such a system of connections is self-contained. It is sufficient, eternal and productive.

Man has built production as an open system: production begins with the involvement of natural resources, and they do not return back to nature. The vast majority of the items that have served a man are thrown out to them by a dump. Such a system is open both at the input and at the output. Such systems can exist for a long time only in small sizes. If production grows, sooner or later it comes into conflict with the principle that life on Earth is based on - the principle of a closed system. At present, it is required that humanity as soon as possible passes from an open system of links between social production and the environment to a closed system. If this does not happen, horrific consequences await us. The human habitat was formed long before its appearance as a biological species. Therefore, a person cannot adapt to an environment of a different quality. Even minor changes in the chemical composition of air, water and food cause irreversible disturbances in the body of the thinking, regardless of gender and age, nationality and size of capital. American ecologist Louis Battan said this well in the 1970s: "One of two things: either people will make less smoke on the Earth or smoke will make people on Earth less." To overcome the ecological crisis created by man, he must solve at least three problems. First, it is necessary to preserve the maximum of natural ecosystems that control the quality of the human habitat as the youngest species that cannot adapt to a different environment. Secondly, to create an industry of non-waste production for life support of the ever growing population of the planet; Thirdly: to solve the problem of effective recycling of human waste to compensate for losses in the biological cycle.

But as practice has shown, governments do not attach much importance to what does not bring instant profit. Developed countries in the world spend on environmental protection no more than 1-2% of the gross national product (Japan with 15% of GNP is, rather, an exception). Calculations show that the average annual value of economic damage due to environmental pollution is now in different countries from 3 to 5% of the gross national product. It is quite obvious that the economy at the expense of nature, the desire to solve the tasks of today, ignoring the requirements for preserving the usefulness of natural systems, is a path that will lead to huge losses in the near future and to even greater losses in the far future.

It seems that the national institutions of power solve only narrowly directed, disjointed tasks of improving the quality of life without having a common strategy and development plans. This task is imposed on the shoulders of only a few enthusiasts, often surrounded by a dense veil of silence and ostracism.

Known only to a narrow circle of the Internet community, a brilliant futurist and designer from the USA Jacques Fresco offers a real way to a fundamentally new level of development with the help of the technological systems developed by him. In its center named "Project Venus", he developed and applied in practice models of innovative multi-level ring cities that combine the most advanced materials and construction methods. Giving preference to circular forms, the engineer was guided by models taken from nature. Indeed, the circle (ball) is a universal and widespread form both at the macro level (galaxy, planet) and micro-level (the shape of the skull structure of a person, flower, etc.) Assuming that the periphery of the city is occupied with production (food , products), and the center - scientific work, recreation, cultural, sporting events, etc., then from the point of view of ergonomics and design this option remains the most optimal and economical, facilitating the work of urban infrastructure and communications. This model is most in line with the concept of building "closed type" systems.

And this is not the only attempt. In 1995, the scientists' forecasts were, as a rule, pessimistic, regarding the prospects for the development of human civilization. The response to this was the official establishment of the Global Ecovillage Network (GEN), recognized as a UN consultant over time. Its tasks were to unite and support the rural and urban communities in the formation of a high-quality lifestyle based on environmental knowledge. GEN began to establish interaction between politicians, scientists, entrepreneurs and eco-communities, implementing the strategy of a global transition to sustainable development. In 1998, the practice of creating eco-settlements for the first time was officially included by the United Nations in the list of 100 best practices of sustainable lifestyles.

By the time GEN was founded, some countries had already accumulated a certain experience in creating eco-trees. Since the 1930s, in different parts of the world (Iceland, Scotland, USA, Sri Lanka, Burkina Faso, etc.), these settlements arose to unite people with a certain worldview and common spiritual values. The most famous were the eco-settlements of Auroville in southern India, founded in 1968, and Arcosanti in Arizona (USA, 1970).

Curiously, the town-planning concept of Auroville as a model of the universal "city of the future", designed for 50,000 inhabitants, also echoes some of Jacques Fresco's ideas. It was designed for a deserted area on the basis of a sketch of the inspiration of the settlement of Mirra Alfass. The concept of settlement was based on the idea of universal unity. In the center of the territory was a park, and on the main square a spiritual center was built - the Mother Temple. From here spiral trajectories develop the main functional zones of Auroville - residential, cultural, international and industrial. Thanks to this geometry, the layout of the settlement resembles a circular pattern of the Galaxy. The Government of India in 1988 supported the development of Auroville as a future research center in the areas of integrating urban and rural development strategies, reforestation, land development, water conservation, rainwater harvesting, construction technologies, energy conservation, etc. The project was repeatedly endorsed by UNESCO.

Another ecosettlement, called Arcosanti, has become for many years an experimental and demonstration platform for the introduction of technologies called "Architectural ecology". The term, the idea of realization and the basic concepts of "arkology" were introduced into professional use and belong to the famous American architect of Italian origin Paolo Soleri. Over some period of time, approximately three-quarters of the original design intent was implemented, which has undergone numerous changes during the implementation. Planning is carried out by the Arcosanti Planning and Development Department. He applies certain principles of "arkology" in the work, such as multifunctional use of space, compactness, pedestrian accessibility and necessary comfort of households, restriction of building density, minimization of resource consumption, use of solar energy, etc. Here, internship programs and workshops for designers are held, In educational and cultural programs. Since the beginning of the experiment, more than 7,000 volunteers have taken part in them.

The concept of constructing "closed cycle" systems is possible and necessary to realize not only at the level of cities and settlements, but also separately taken houses (homesteads) of the generic type. I do not accidentally consider the "generic" construction of elements of society - in this case, the continuity of generations is very important. In such house, while maintaining the established connections, it is absolutely necessary to think about the possibility of system "upgrade" open to innovations and improvements. Therefore, all the knowledge and materials described in the previous chapters without a bundle are completely useless - they are similar to the details of an engine that is dismantled. In an attempt to assemble this puzzle piece, I present to you the following scheme, which may need further research, additions and different construction options:

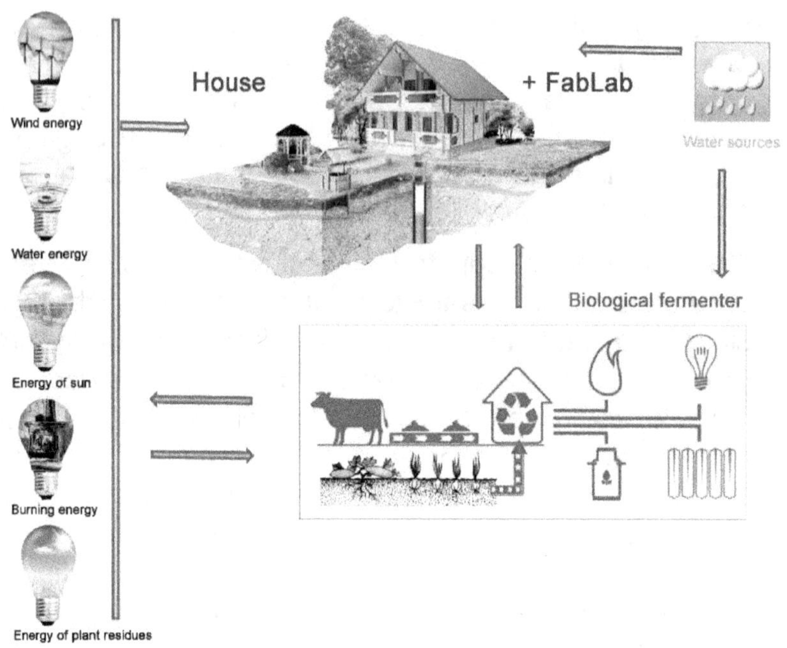

All the farm on the scheme is divided into four main blocks and one additional (home workshop):

A) Housing block with the home workshop "fab-lab" (see Chapter 2) for the production of basic necessities (including utensils, interior, furniture, clothes, etc.) The meaning of this "duet" is very simple - the more you produce at home, the less money you spend in the store;

B) The first power unit, which produces heat and electricity. Emphasis is placed on renewable energy sources. If you live near a forest, dead wood in the form of fuel can also be considered a renewable source (see chapter 3,4);

C) The second power unit (water supply), which supplies technical and drinking water for the needs of the family. All water resources are sorted into two types. Technical water (rainwater, meltwater, water reservoirs and the dew point (see Chapter 4) and the other is freed from mechanical impurities in the prefilters and used for washing, showering, sewage and cleaning. Drinking water can also be obtained from the technical - but requires filters of finer purification for this;

D) The third power unit supplies food and materials - these are vegetable gardens, plantations and a garden, pets and livestock - everything that was useful for a person and his household initially. The intermediate fermenter (household unit for biogas production - see Chapter 4) serves as the intermediate node between the living and food blocks. It utilizes waste and supplies fertilizers to the plantations, plus combustible biogas into the house.

Ideally, such a family estate should be capable of locating in any part of the land, even if it was not adapted to people's lives before (for example, the desert that emerged from the technical exploitation of the land, etc.). This implies, first of all, compact installations for the extraction of basic resources - heat, electricity, water and food, assembled from simple units, replacement parts with a simple assembly manual. All households must be self-contained, be economical and not harmful for the environment.

Of course, solving such problems is a matter of a distant future, but the person who has solved this problem will open a new chapter and an entire industry for the needs of self-sufficient farms (consumables, upgrade, maintenance, etc.) This will raise the independence and freedom of the individual to a completely new level, contributing to a more complete disclosure of its creativity. But this requires the policy of a more enlightened state - using in its activity not an abstract and vague concept of "people", but a more concrete and understandable "Family and Man".

The end of the second part

***Bonus**: articles of different authors:*

__Ritual Saxena (India):__
__"Ergonomics"__

What is Ergonomics?

Ergonomics is the art and science of designing or arranging spaces, products and systems so as to facilitate the people using them. It can be a well designed kitchen, home, work space, a workstation, a chair, a desk, a rack or a storage space. Basically, ergonomics is applying design to anything used by people to enhance health and safety of the spaces they occupy or use; this in sports and leisure, too.

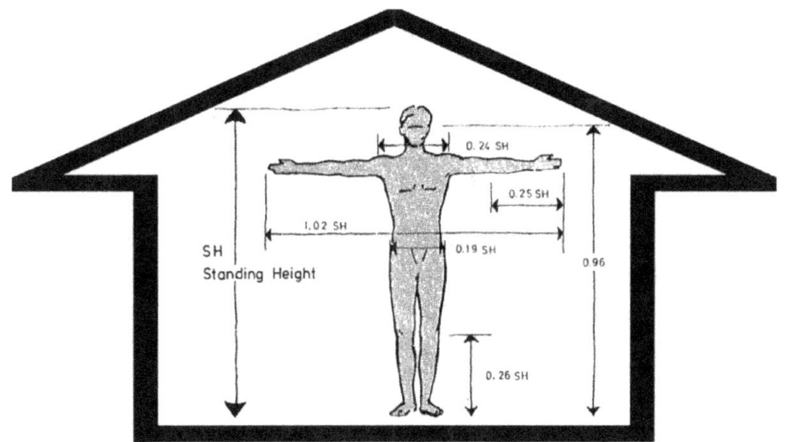

The approximate dimensions around which ergonomic spaces are built

Why Ergonomics?

The idea behind applying ergonomics is to help better posture, performance and reduce stress and strain. It allows a better interaction between the human, the space, the products within the space, the system and environment.

Ergonomics allows for right posture and product

design

Ergonomics is applied everywhere be it a seat for office, for railway carriage, airplanes, forklifts, etc. Or a commercial kitchen, a crane cabin design, locomotive, supermarket, ship and plane interiors. Ergonomics is also used to modify rehabilitation equipment emergency room designs and layouts, industrial trucks, trolley designs, warehouse design and search and rescue operations room. You think of a space and using it - you will be applying ergonomics.

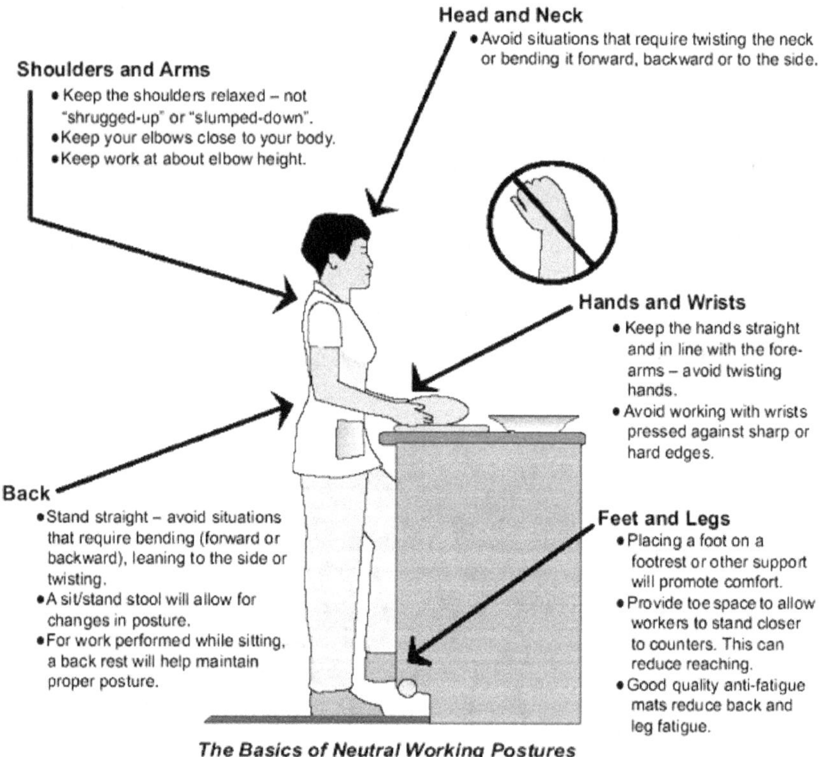

The Basics of Neutral Working Postures

Ergonomic design at supermarket counter

Ergonomics is practiced at home and work because it occupies less space, requires less resources to make and we get more out of less of space and resources. Work related injuries and illnesses cost companies billions of dollars in insurance. Lower back pain is the most common work related disability that affects most employees due to incorrectly designed chairs and desks.

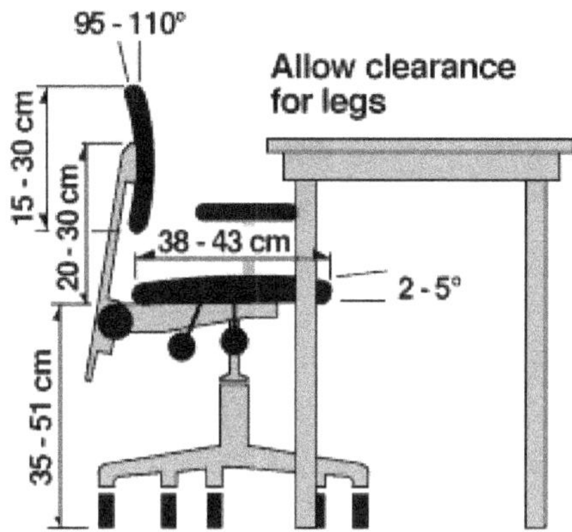

An ergonomically designed office chair

Ergonomics helps create productive and comfortable work spaces where human limitations and abilities are taken into account while designing the space. This includes accommodating the body size, the skill, speed, strength, abilities, and attitudes of the people. Ergonomics also considers the age of the person while designing space, services, systems and equipment such as the transport system, building facilities, and living spaces.

A bus designed with a ramp for wheelchairs and gurneys

How ergonomics work?

This field of study originated in the 1950s. The etymology of the word is the Greek word - *ergon that means* work', and aims to describe the pattern of *economics* that goes into doing a task. It means the economy of body movement, use of space, effort, convenience, etc. Ergonomics relies research on various scientific areas of knowledge like anatomy, morphology, physiology, psychology, engineering, etc; that contribute to the design and functionality.

Cooking is a social and relaxing activity thus the space is designed keeping the psychology in mind

- o Biomechanics: the study of muscles and how they are used, as levers, the strength they possess, the force that's required to do work.

- o Anthropometry: the size, shape, of the bodies, including population and variations the space may have to handle

- o Applied psychology: the skills and learning required or may bring and what errors may be possible depending on the difference in the users

- o Social psychology: the kind and size of the group, the dynamics in the group, their learning behavior, communication, etc contribute to ergonomics of a space.

- o Environment and its effect on the user: factors such as radiation, heat, cold, light, noise, vibration, etc contribute to ergonomic design

- o Anatomy and physiology: the bodys own sytems respond to a space through various senses such as vision, smell, hearing and other sensations

Ergonomics works with the above disciplines to achieve the perfect design, data and techniques from several disciplines are brought together to make the perfect design.

Dr. Simon Bashkirov (Belarus): "Transforming solar energy into electricity: Past, Present and Future of Photovoltaics"

Sun has always been and remains practically the only source of energy consumed by the Earth's biosphere, including man. Being at the bottom of food chains, plants use solar energy in the process of photosynthesis, resulting in the formation of nutrients for all other organisms. Phytoplankton using the energy of Sun restores atmospheric oxygen and absorbs excess of carbon dioxide, so that living organisms can breathe. Solar energy causes the evaporation of water from the surface of seas and oceans, initiating the water cycle in nature and determining the climate. Water condenses and falls in the precipitation form feeding rivers and providing water to plants and animals.

After death, the biological material, together with accumulated sun energy in chemical form, transforms into hydrocarbon energy carriers: oil and gas. The energy of water flow used in hydroelectric power stations and the wind used in wind farms are also largely due to the Sun. Thus, the primal source of all energy resources (nuclear fuel is the only exception) used by man for the production of electric power is directly or indirectly the Sun.

As it is known from physics, the more stages the solar energy passes on the path of transformation into electricity, the greater part of it is dissipated in the form of heat. Therefore, obviously, the most rational way of using solar energy is its direct conversion to electricity. The devices for such a transformation are called "solar cells", and the field of science and technology on the development of these devices and the entire technology of the direct light conversion to electricity is generally called "photovoltaics". Typically, solar cells are made in the form of thin plates with an area of 10*10 square centimeters. For the industrial production of electricity or for providing energy to large objects, solar cells are assembled into so-called photovoltaic modules with an area of about one square meter, of which solar batteries are then built, the area of which is measured in tens of square meters.

Solar cells were invented quite recently. The principle of the action of the solar cell is based on the so-called photoelectric effect, a phenomenon discovered in 1839 by Alexander Becquerel and actively researched since the second half of the 19th century by such scientists as H. Hertz, A. Stoletov, F. Lenard, A. Einstein. Note that Albert Einstein received the Nobel Prize for his work on the theory of photoelectric effect but not for his famous relativity theory, which was initially met by the scientific community with some distrust.

The essence of the photoelectric effect is that particles of light (photons) acting on some substances and materials knock out the electric current carriers (electrons) from their surface. By assembling in a specific design a pair of materials with different initial electron concentrations, you can get a device that emits constant voltage under the light action, like a battery. The photoelectric effect is manifested in electrolytes, metals and semiconductors, such as silicon.

Silicon is known today like the main material for microelectronics. It is silicon that produces radio components, chips for computer processors, mobile phones and all modern electronic devices. And from silicon in 1954 specialists of Bell Laboratories developed the first industrial solar cells for electricity production. The development belongs to three employees of the company - Calvin Souther Fuller, Daryl Chapin and Gerald Pearson. However, ideas and the first prototypes of solar batteries appeared much earlier, at the turn of the 19th and 20th centuries, and they belonged to the outstanding Italian chemist of Armenian origin Giacomo Chamichanu.

Giacomo developed the first prototypes of photoelectric converters of chemical type. This is how Chimichan described the future of world energy in the year of 1912 at the 8th International Congress on Applied Chemistry: *"Industrial colonies without smoking pipes will arise on arid lands; The forests of glass tubes will spread in the plains, and glass buildings will grow everywhere; There will be photochemical processes that until now were an unknown mystery of plants, but all this will be mastered by human civilization, which will know how to get even more abundant fruits .... And if in the near future the coal reserves are completely exhausted, the civilization will not disappear, but will exist as long as Sun shines!"* Of course, in those years of the world wars and totalitarian governments, it was impossible to realize the ideas of wide-scale implementation of solar energy, and Chamichan was forced to investigate chemical weapons and protection from it. As a result, he got poisoning, from which he did not recover until his death, and ideas of using the solar energy were put off until better times.

Anyway, half a century after Chamichan's report, interest in using solar energy has increased dramatically. This was promoted, among other things, by the space development and the need to search for the optimal source of energy for space ships. Already in 1958, the United States launched the first satellite using solar panels - Avangard-1. In the same year, few months later, satellite using solar batteries to generate energy was also launched in the USSR, - Sputnik-3.

In the 1960s, age of hippies, rock'n'roll and tube amplifiers, the silicon industry was at the earliest stages of its formation. Therefore, solar cells based on massive silicon crystals were extremely expensive. At that time, so-called *first generation* of solar cells was developed, the main feature of which was the use of bulk semiconductor crystals of large size. The production process of these materials at that time was laborious and expensive, but space exploration - in this field mainly the first-generation solar cells were used - always required high costs, and this was not taken into account. Along with silicon, in the solar cells of the first generation, crystals of gallium arsenide were also used - compounds of one of the rarest metals (gallium) with one of the most toxic nonmetals (arsenic). Very "environmentally friendly", isn't it? However, for limited use in space, this was perfectly acceptable, since gallium arsenide is ideal absorbing material for the solar spectrum.

Electricity produced by first generation solar cells was expensive. To install one watt of power it was required to spend 4-5 US dollars. For example, for a full-fledged electricity supply to an apartment, a maximum power of 2000 watts and a daily average of at least 100 watts are required. Thus, for the normal equipment of the apartment with solar modules of the first generation, it was necessary to spend up to ten thousand dollars. In addition, the elements of the first generation had a low efficiency coefficient, i.e. low percentage of the incoming solar energy converted into an electrical (usually one-tenth). Consequently, large area batteries should be used to ensure the required power. To provide one apartment, a photovoltaic installation of tens of square meters was needed! Not mentioning the fact that bulk crystals of silicon and gallium arsenide, and therefore solar cells based on them, are quite fragile.

 It is quite natural that, as a result of all of the above, the first generation solar cells could not find wide application anywhere excepting the space. No one seriously thought about large-scale use of them on Earth. Everything changed after the creation of the technology of so-called thin-film solar cells. Their appearance marked the beginning of the *second generation* in photovoltaics. In the thin-film solar cells, as the name suggests, instead of bulk semiconductor crystals, thin films deposited on a special substrate are used. The thickness of such films is usually of micrometers (compare with the cells of the first generation based on silicon crystals of millimeter thickness). The appearance of thin-film cells has solved a number of problems inherent in the first generation solar cells:

- o Material consumption: Thin-film solar cells require thousands times less semiconductor material, because they are thousands times thinner.
- o The problem of fragility: unlike crystals, thin-film cells are less fragile.
- o Semiconductor quality requirements: generally, quality requirements for thin films are usually lower than for semiconductor crystals. Therefore, they are easier to make.
- o Flexibility: flexible solar cells can be made of thin-film materials on substrates made of plastic and metal foil, which opens wide prospects for their use in a wide variety of areas. Bulk silicon crystals cannot be made flexible.
- o As a consequence of the first items, low cost and high commercial attractiveness of thin-film solar cells take place.

Since the 1990s, the active expansion of the second generation solar cells to the photovoltaic markets began. The efficiency of these cells (the percentage of solar energy conversion into electrical energy) soon reached the parameters of the first generation elements, and then, in some cases, even exceeded them.

The flagship of the second generation solar cells became CIGS (copper, indium, gallium and sulfur compounds) thin films based devices. The process of manufacturing a CIGS-based thin film solar cell looks like the following.

1. At the first stage it is necessary to deposit a conductive layer onto the substrate (glass, plastic). On the glass substrates a conductive layer of molybdenum metal is usually deposited. This metal is characterized by high thermal and chemical resistance, and not corroding in the subsequent stages of the solar cell manufacturing. Molybdenum deposition onto the glass usually is performed with the help of a magnetron - a device that in its operating principle resembles a microwave oven.

2. In the second stage, the metals (copper, indium and gallium) must be deposited onto the molybdenum layer. Metals can be deposited layer by layer or simultaneously, for example, by spraying the alloy with a magnetron or by co-precipitation from a solution. The metal film

obtained on the surface of molybdenum at this stage is called a "precursor".

3. Then the precursors are sent to the furnace, where they are annealed at high temperature (usually about 400-500 °C) in sulfur vapor. As a result of a number of chemical reactions, a CIGS semiconductor is formed, which, in many properties and interaction with light, is similar to silicon.

4. Then the additional layers are deposited onto the CIGS surface, usually transparent conductive materials, for example zinc oxide. These layers are needed to effectively separate positive and negative electrical charges.

5. And in the final stage, an upper contact is deposited - tracks made of metal, for example, aluminum.

Solar cells, obtained by this technology, can convert to electricity up to 20% of the incident solar energy. In addition to CIGS, second-generation solar cells used thin films of cadmium telluride, as well as polycrystalline (consisting of a large number of small crystalline) silicon films. The cost of 1 watt of installed capacity with the use of thin-film of the second generation solar cells fell to 1 dollar, which made it quite feasible for large-scale use of solar energy for domestic and industrial needs. Fantasy became a reality, and Giacomo Chamichan's ideas were implemented.

Nevertheless, second generation solar cells have a number of significant drawbacks, the main of which is the need in rare metals (indium, gallium), as well as toxic components (cadmium). At the moment, the efforts of researchers around the world are aimed at finding new materials that can solve this problem. Solar cells that will not contain toxic and rare components, while being thin-film, flexible and highly efficient, will form *the third generation* of photovoltaics. An important feature of the third generation solar cells is also a departure from expensive and complex vacuum technologies for obtaining materials for cheap methods of "wet chemistry".

A huge work, starting from 1990s, was done by the group of Prof. Katagiri of Nagaoka National College of Technology and their followers. The idea was to replace the rare and expensive indium and gallium in CIGS with much more affordable zinc and tin. As a result, a new semiconductor material CZTS (copper-zinc-tin-sulfate) was created. Otherwise it was supposed to preserve technology completely similar to the production of solar cells based on CIGS, which should simplify the procedure for switching to this new material. Over the next fifteen years, active work was done to optimize and adapt technologies, resulting in 2010 in solar cells CZTS-based having struck 10% threshold of efficiency, which is a conditional frontier to the market. In the near future, solar cells based on CZTS will begin to be actively introduced into industrial stations and household installations.

 In addition to CZTS, the promising materials for third generation photovoltaics include organic solar cells with so-called dye-sensitized cells, as well as cells based on amorphous (glass-like) silicon films. Among dye-sensitized solar cells, special attention should be paid to the so-called "perovskite" solar cells based on hybrid organic-inorganic compounds with the perovskite structure. In 2012-2013, these unusual solar cells have made a real breakthrough, demonstrating unprecedented for any other technology progress in increasing efficiency. For a few years perovskite solar cells have come a way, for the passage of which other photovoltaic materials took years and dozens of years. The extraordinary combination of physical properties of perovskites allowed them to increase the efficiency of energy conversion of solar cells on their basis during 2012-2013 from 7% to 16%. As you can see, for a short time it was possible to create samples of perovskite solar cells with performance characteristics that exceed those for most other thin-film solar cells of the third generation, whose technologies were developed for decades. After a while, perovskite solar cells reached the efficiency of sunlight conversion into electricity by more than 20%.

The architecture of the perovskite solar cells is inverse to the architecture of traditional thin-film cells of the second generation. As a substrate and a transparent contact, industrial glass with a transparent conductive layer (ITO, FTO) is usually applied. Such glasses are produced in large quantities and are widely used as transparent contacts in microelectronics, for example in modern liquid crystal displays. The process of manufacturing a perovskite solar cell can be described as fallowing:

1. On the underlay, the so-called "photoanode" is deposited - a nanostructured porous transparent material based on titanium, zirconium or zinc oxides. To apply it, you can use already familiar magnetron, or you can use wet chemistry

methods, for example electrochemical deposition or sol-gel.

2. Then a layer of an organometallic compound with a perovskite structure is deposited to the photoanode by wet chemistry methods. For this such deposition methods as spin-coating, rolling printing, inkjet printing, etc. can be used.

3. Then a buffer layer (photocell) and an upper opaque metal contact are deposited onto the perovskite surface.

It is significantly that only wet chemistry methods in obtaining perovskitnye solar cells are used at all stages. All processes are carried out under mild conditions without the use of strong fields, vacuum, high temperatures, etc. All this highly corresponds to the paradigm of the third generation solar cells.

Like the previous two generations, the third generation of photovoltaics is not without shortcomings. The common drawback of third-generation devices is the insufficiently high efficiency of converting light into electricity, as it is in the case of solar cells based on CZTS, or, as in the case of perovskite, poor stability of characteristics. The problems of precisely perovskite solar cells should also include the need to use expensive synthetic substances as a material for buffer layers, as well as the need to make upper contacts of gold. However, there is a reason to believe that in the near future these problems will be solved. Russian scientists of Prof. Gladyshev's group are actively working on finding alternative cheap buffer layers for perovskite solar cells, which should make them competitive on the photovoltaic market.

In addition to CZTS and perovskites, there are many interesting materials, on which hopes are placed and in which scientists and engineers see solutions to existing problems of photovoltaics. Many consider very promising and environmentally friendly so-called fully oxide solar cells whose active layers consist only of metals and oxygen. A large number of works are devoted to solar cells based on tin sulfide (tin and sulfur compound). A huge number of materials are actively explored but remains in the shadows since solar cells based on these materials have not overcome the ten percent efficiency barrier. Anyway, the third generation solar cells undoubtedly belong to the near future.

Technology, however, does not stand still and every day small and big discoveries are made. Photovoltaics continue to evolve, and many generations of solar cells are waiting for us. Sooner or later, the development of the third generation will be completed, and its technology will go to the industry. The development of the fourth generation of photovoltaic will begin. Perhaps, the fourth generation solar cells will not be produced in factories, but will be sold in the form of separate components (as a set of aerosols), with which everyone will be able make himself a solar cell of the required shape and size by spraying the components on any surfaces, like graffiti. Who knows what technologies are waiting for us in the Future.

Today, solar energy has fully proved its worth. The average daily flux of solar energy in the southern latitudes is approximately three hundred watt per square meter. Considering the level of the World energy production (about 20 thousand terawatts per year), it can be estimated that at 25% efficiency of solar energy conversion, a site of only 30,000 square kilometers will suffice for the total energy supply of the planet. Today, the price per one kilowatt-hour for industrial generation of electricity with the help of solar cells is averagely of 0.25 euro. According to the European Association of Photovoltaic (EPIA), by 2020 the average cost of electricity produced by photovoltaics will decrease to less than 0.1 euro per one kilowatt-hour for industrial installations and less than 0.15 euro per one kilowatt-hour for installations in residential buildings.

Yet in 2013, the price of one kilowatt-hour in the regions with a large amount of Sun (North Africa or Southern California) was less than 0.10 euro, and in some regions up to 0.06 euro To compare, in Eastern Europe, electricity tariffs for the private final consumers range from 0.05 to 0.09 euro per 1 one kilowatt-hour. Thus, it is expected that by 2020 the cost of "solar" electricity for final consumers will become competitive with the energy from the traditional energy source.

The total capacity of the implemented photovoltaic plants is increasing exponentially from year to year. At the beginning of 2014, the total capacity of installations operating in the whole World reached 139 gigawatt (139 billion watts), while in 2000 this figure was only 1.4 gigawatt. Only in 2013, 39 gigawatt of photovoltaic power were installed in the World. The world leaders in the capacity of solar energy plants are Germany and Italy (32% and 16% of the global capacity, respectively). Speaking about the outlook for the next few years, optimistic forecasts, in view of the depletion of reserves and the reduction of hydrocarbon consumption, by 2050 photovoltaic will provide from 25 to 80 percent of the

World's total energy consumption. Taking into account these numbers, solar energy can hardly be called "alternative" or "not traditional." In the 21th century, solar energy will become the main source of electricity on Earth, and after the general transition to electric vehicles and the abandonment of internal combustion engines the era of industrial dominance of hydrocarbons will end.

Finally, let's talk about how to make solar panel from commercially available materials and components in order to provide electricity to your house with your own hands.

For work we need: a set of solar cells (sold at Aliexpress), glass plates, aluminum or steel frames, sealant, metal foil strip for soldering, soldering iron (better soldering station), solder, electronic multimeter.

Our homemade solar module will consist of solar cells laid out on a glass plate and connected in series (plus to minus) with a foil strip. Since the elements are connected in series, it is very important that all of them are working. A non-working (pierced) element will not generate a current and in a consecutive chain of elements it will hang as "ballast", not producing but consuming energy and lowering the total power. Therefore, the first step is to check all solar cells immediately after unpacking them. For testing, you can use a simple household multimeter in the voltage measurement mode and an ordinary table lighter lamp. If the element emits a stable voltage when illuminated by the lamp according to the nominal value (usually 0.5-1.5 volts), then it is working good. If there is no voltage or it decreases rapidly, this is a spoilage. Such elements cannot be used in our homemade module.

In the second stage, it is necessary to solder the strips of metal tape to the rear contact of the solar cells. If you have enough experience in radio engineering, you can use a soldering iron, but there is a risk of overheating and disabling solar cells, since the soldering iron normally gives off a very high temperature. It is much more reliable to use a temperature-controlled soldering station. Use low-melting high-quality solder based on modern tin alloys. It will ensure reliable contact with minimal overheating of the elements. Pay attention: tin and other alloys lose their mechanical properties at negative temperatures (the so-called "tin plague"). If you plan to use your solar panel, in frosty winter (or at Arctic/Antarctic), make sure that the solder you use to braze the elements is frost-resistant.

After the cells are soldered, it is necessary to check them again with a multimeter and a lamp, as described above. After that, working cells must be spread out and glued to the glass plate with the front surface facing upwards. The free ends of the strips of conductive tape, soldered to the rear contacts of the cells, must be then placed above the upper contacts of the next cells. To these upper contacts now they must be soldered. As a result, the elements must be connected in series. The voltage produced by them with this type of connection will be summarized together. Thus, a self-made module of two hundred (10*20) one volt cells will give us a total voltage of 200 V.

After the glue has dried and our cells are securely fastened to the rear plate, it is necessary to close them with the upper glass plate and seal the module. All this is necessary in order to protect solar cells from the negative impact of the environmental factors. Dust, wind, rain, atmospheric oxygen - all these can quickly bring our homemade solar module into disrepair in case of poor sealing quality.

Ideally, as a top layer you need to use special glass that transmits light in a wide spectral range, including infra-red and ultraviolet. The problem is that a conventional window glass "cuts off" part of the solar spectrum, and as a result, a large percentage of the incident energy is converted into heat, but not into electricity. One of the most interesting ways to solve this problem is the use of glass with a specially designed luminescent coating. This coating transforms the invisible solar ultraviolet light into a well-transmitted by glass visible radiation, which is then absorbed by the solar cells. This approach allows a several percent increase in the solar energy conversion efficiency of our homemade module. However, in the absence of such a special glass, you can dispense with the usual window glass.

Next, the sealed module is assembled into a metal frame, soldered to the pins for the connection to the network and everything is ready to go. It remains only to mount it on a well-illuminated surface, for example on the roof or the wall of your building. The module can be monitored using a multimeter. If you want to fully provide your apartment with electricity form solar energy, one module may not be enough. You may need to make a battery of several modules. If each module outputs voltage enough big, then you can connect the modules in the battery in parallel type of connection (plus to plus, minus to minus). With this connection scheme, the battery will give out voltage value as from one module, but the current (amperes) and, consequently, the power will be summarized. However, one should remember and understand that the solar battery produces a direct current (as in car batteries), while the most household appliances are designed for the use of alternating current, as in a conventional network. Therefore, if you want to power from a solar battery such devices as a refrigerator or a washing machine you will need additional equipment, in particular a DC to AC converter. In addition, since in cloudy weather the illumination of the panels is continuously changing, it is necessary to use voltage stabilizers and accumulators, used as a buffer and storage for the generated electricity. It is easy to find all this stuff on sale, for example on Aliexpress.

If you do not want to risk making the panel with your own hands, you can always buy ready-made panels of any size, power and configuration for any purpose and task of any scale. In addition, nowadays there are a lot of companies that can design, manufacture and install on the turn-key project the panels of the required configuration for an individual project tailor-made for your needs.

Yesterday we could read and about solar panels on the streets and roofs of houses only be in fantastic futuristic novels, and it was just like a crazy dream. Today we see them in our cities and we are already getting used to it. Tomorrow our grandchildren will fully cover their need for electricity from the solar energy and they probably will think that it has always been so.

The end